Ed Oates instigated the project and received the backing of the Marazion and District Forum and procured funding from the Heritage Lottery. His idea was that the memories and recollections of the people of the area should be preserved and that by doing so the project could promote a better understanding between the generations and bring the community together.

John Pollard was appointed co-ordinator in January 2005 and volunteers were recruited throughout the two-year project.

Reminiscence work was already underway in Cornwall, led by Dr Gary Tregidga of the Cornwall Audio Visual Archive, part of the University of Exeter Institute of Cornish Studies. Locally there were projects at Pendeen (Geevor), Porthcurno and St. Ives all of whom offered advice and support.

CAVA provided our trainer and mentor, Dr. Mandy Morris who brought a wealth of experience of the field from the University of Leicester and her work in the Midlands.

So …..

We started to collect and record people's memories.

We put together an archive of recordings to be kept at the Cornish Studies Library, Redruth and Marazion Museum

We worked with all age groups – from 3 year olds to 93 year olds!!

We felt privileged to listen to the stories and received total support from everyone.

We wrote this book…

Published by
Marazion & District Forum
Marazion, Cornwall

Printed by
Headland Printers, Penzance, Cornwall

All rights reserved
© Marazion & District Forum

ISBN 978-0-9555618-0-1

Introduction

The story of how the Marazion Memories project was created is a story almost as long as the project itself. For anyone who hasn't run a volunteer project, as I hadn't in 2002, the journey is a voyage of discovery – there's no telling what is around the next corner. But the message I want to pass on is that even though it takes time and thought to put all the necessary parts in place it really is possible to plan, finance and run a volunteer project. So what are you waiting for? Give it a go!

It's now 2am on a January night in 2004. The post Christmas blues are with me and I'm about to start module two of an eight module part time Masters degree course. To make things feel worse I'm about to start a week of lectures on Statistics – not my strongest subject at any time and a skill not used for a decade. I've just finished the application form for a grant from the Heritage Lottery Fund. The questions on the form ask why the project is being run, who will benefit and how. The questions are general questions and it takes some time to think of answers that are specific to the project and will best illustrate the main features of the project. I've been working on the form for the last four hours, carefully selecting words and phrases from the project plan. The Heritage Lottery Fund, I hope is going to be the main funding source and if this application isn't accepted then the project won't run. There's a clear sense of relief now that it's done and at last I can close my eyes. Tomorrow it will go in the post, and the Statistics lectures will start.

Two years before, in 2002 I was at one of the early meetings of the Marazion and District Forum. We had had talks from various people to help set the Forum on its feet, but as yet there hadn't been any decision on what projects should be run. I'd suggested that we might like to start an oral history project, and having suggested it I was then required to put the plan together. The research and planning started. The usual chapters on the aims and objectives of the project, financial plans, risk assessments and how it was going to be managed were in there. It ended up with a project plan running to sixty pages. It had been reviewed by the Forum and only then it was agreed that it was ready to go out for consideration by funding agencies.

Writing the project plan was slow progress fitting in with the day job, studying and family life. Enthusiasm was difficult to maintain throughout that planning period, and I'm grateful for the gentle prodding and enquiring by the Forum members as they kept me on track and added ideas and amendments. It must have seemed like I would never get there, I sometimes wondered that myself.

The letter from Penwith District Council agreeing to fund the training needs of the project was a great boost to everyone's enthusiasm. But the letter from the Heritage Lottery Fund agreeing to support the project was the greatest moment. It was recognition that the Forum's plan was thorough and confirmation that we really could do something for the benefit of the four parishes. At the same time I knew that there were lots more to do. It was another year before the job of Marazion Memories Co-ordinator was to be filled. Placing the advert, forming the interview panel and reviewing the completed application forms all took time. The three year journey to the beginning of the project had been a voyage of discovery. The super people that I'd met, the encouragement, support and great ideas from so many, the wonderful feeling of bringing a community project together had all been part of the journey. Now the really exciting times were about to start. This 'ship' had been built and with the Project Co-ordinator at the helm it was launched – would it float?

The production of the book and the CD, in 2009 is the culmination of this project. These and the web site www.marazion-memories.co.uk will live on after the end of the project, and I hope that all those, young and old who took part in the project will carry their own memories of the project with them through life.

Enormous amounts of thanks and praise go to the Project Co-ordinator as he has steered the project for the past two years. Also thank you to the contributors and volunteers who gave their time, talents and memories. Enjoy the written and recorded memories.

Ed Oates.

Contents

The Project	1
Introduction	3-4
Contents	5
St Hilary	7
Perranuthnoe	9
Ludgvan	11
Marazion	13

PERSONAL MEMORIES

John Allen	16
Peter Badcock	18
Roy and Muriel Badcock	20
Howard Curnow	22
George Curnow	24
Arnold Derrington	26
Mary Brigid Greenwood Penny	28
John and Molly Jago	30
Sid Hayes	32
Gill Joyce	34
Myra Kitchen	36
Howard King	38
Anne Laity	41
Benny Lugg	42
Herbert Phillips	44
Zena Row	46
Pauline & Alfred John Rowe	48
Bill Sewell	50
Isabel Thomas	52
Godfrey Varker	54
Marie Vellanoweth	56
Father Walke	58

THEMES

The Second World War	60
1942 – Enemy attack on Marazion	63
School	65
The Mount	74
Growing Up	79

ST HILARY

From the Radio Times of 16th December 1927:

'Bethlehem in Cornwall' by Bernard Walke, Vicar of St. Hilary's Marazion. Listeners to London and Daventry will have an opportunity on Tuesday, December 20, of hearing again the Christmas play, 'Bethlehem', which was broadcast last year from St. Hilary. ...You who sit listening by your fireside must picture to yourselves a lighted church, gay with the decorations of the coming festival, where actors sing and pray as though they were about the ordinary business of life, the tilling of the soil and the tending of cows...It is to this end that 'Bethlehem' is acted again at St. Hilary this Christmas time, that we who take part and you who listen so far away, may together enter more deeply into the mystery of Christmas.

This is a picture of Relubbus Carnival! We have learned what a small but very active community this was, again before the days when the road was so busy. The Chapel was a focus of life, the river provided work for the tin streamers but also regularly flooded and Tea Treats and Carnivals provided the opportunity for 'special' days.

This is a parish of huge contrasts which reflect the whole 'Cornish' way of life. The fishermen on the coast with their huts and communal boiler for crabs and lobsters The Mines throughout the parish with their workings and associated the tin streams. Farming of every description and the variety of landscapes, soils and working conditions. Isolated communities, little hamlets and the scattered chapels all over the parish. The Parish Church at the centre of the life of the area, with its intriguing history.

The school – we have recorded many stories of the long walk to and from school, the happy times there.

War time in the area – little direct impact but Land Army girls changed many lives – including their own.

St. Hilary Churchtown with at one time a pub then an orphanage and of course the Land Army Hostel.

In all the long history of St Hilary Church, no period was as controversial or as innovative as when Rev Bernard Walke was its vicar. Pilloried for its 'high' church stance with the fabric of the Church attacked by his opponents, Father Walke continued his remarkable ministry travelling the parish on his donkey! He has been described as a most extraordinary man, not the least for his writing of the 'Bethlehem Play' broadcast live from the Church in the 1927 (picture) and 1997.

Traditional St Hilary carols *(preserved from memory by Howard King)*

PERRANUTHNOE

Unbelieveable, but, pre-war the youngsters of the parish would promenade along the main road from Perran Cross Roads on Sunday evenings. It was here you socialised with your friends, met your boyfriends and where many a marriage was made! Try that today!!!!

We have discovered that Perranuthnoe Parish is much more than the village by the sea. The inland areas of the Parish are equally important and the link between Perran and Goldsithney essential. People from Perran village had to go (walk) to Goldsithney for some shops, the garage, entertainment and of course school. However many went the other way for the church and all it offered and of course for the beach. Goldsithney may have been closer to 'civilisation' with its road and links to St. Hilary and Marazion whereas Perranuthnoe, until the mid 20th Century was a farming village with a mining past. Joe Laity and Marie Vellanoweth both gave testimony to the changing structure of village life, as did Iris Brewer, all of whom had been involved in the community when it was a collection of working farms. Mr Laity described:

"I remember Perranuthnoe as a farming village: John Laity's farm at Park-an-Praze was on the left as you entered the village but has now been turned into holiday units. The farmhouse 'Clontarf' still exists. Elm Farm was owned by Mr Bettens and was on the right as you entered the village. Dubban farm was at the top of the village and was farmed by Mr. Jim Laity, his wife and two unmarried brothers. The third farm was farmed by Joe Laity, my grandfather at Lynfield, our present home. His family consisted of 4 daughters and one son, my father William Joseph Laity. The farm below the church was farmed by Mr. Vellanoweth who had two daughters, Peggy and Marie who are both living in the village now. Churchtown Farm buildings still survive and were mentioned in the Domesday Book. Mr Gilbert owned the farm opposite Churchtown, called Uthno-Veor. The yard is still called Gilbert's Yard. After the death of Mr. Gilbert his wife and son and daughter had the house built in the field at the back of the farm buildings, now called 'Lamorna'. The Phillips family farmed Ednovean where they lived and also owned Penalyree House and farm buildings. These were the most modern of all the farm buildings in the village, now converted into dwellings called 'The Mews'. Mr Blight Harvey was a small holder in the village. He owned 3 separate meadows opposite the pub. Thinking back to my schooldays, the farms in Perran would have employed around 28 full time men and kept about 20 horses to work the land."

THE PARISH OF PERRANUTHNOE

Joe Laity, his wife Virginia and daughter Lynn remembered:

When my father William Laity passed the scholarship he had to attend Penzance County School. This meant walking the footpath to Marazion Station where he caught the train to Penzance and then walked again to the school. Wednesday afternoons were kept for sports so he had to attend on Saturday mornings which meant travelling 6 days a week.

The Church bells were rung by Percy Curnow who was a horseman on Johnny Laity's farm in the village. There were 3 bells in the tower and he would pull one with his foot as well as 2 hands. Percy was a village character and had a fishing boat at Boat cove and could often be seen sitting on a bench in front of the shed there, smoking his pipe and having a yarn with the other fishermen. He also kept the Church clock wound up and the graveyard neat and tidy.. Frank Dobson from Goldsithney dug the graves.

The village seat near the Pub was where the men of the village would gather on summer evenings. The main topic of conversation would be what was happening on other farms in the district. One problem the farms had was a shortage of water in the summer because it all had to be carried from Trenow Beach where it came out of the cliff from an adit mine. The men built up this stream so that a 120 gallon barrel could be put on the frame of a farm cart, backed under the stream and pulled by horse to different fields for the cattle to drink. If it was a very dry time the barrel had to be brought to the back of the farmhouse so that all the baths and buckets that were available could be filled. Mains water was brought to the village in 1956!

Joe says:

My Grandmother supplied the people of the village with milk and butter for many years. Of course there were far fewer people living in the village then and they would bring their own jugs and drop them on the dairy table. The milk would be dipped and put in containers after the morning milking at 7a.m., ready in the cool room for collection. Pay Day was Saturdays and people would come to pay for their milk with the takings being counted out into a very old tobacco tin! One lady, Laura Curnow, who lived in Drop Anchor had ½ pint of milk each morning and evening for years because she liked fresh milk. The day came when we had to bottle milk and seal the tops. Virginia and Lynn would dip a 100 bottles of milk a day, before school, to sell to the campsite too.

There are the remains of a stone quarry Trenow which was worked until the 1914 war. The very hard blue elvan stone were removed and taken for the roads which needed repairing. They were tipped by the roadside and men would smash them into the required size with sledge hammers.

Perran and district must have been very busy when the tin mines were working because up to a few years ago from Trebarvah to Marazion there were mine dumps in a row in all the fields. Some of the bigger ones were beside open mineshafts. When more modern machinery became available farmers removed them because they obstructed the use of modern farm implements. Sometimes gravel was crushed from the stones to make concrete blocks which were used to build several houses and bungalows in the area

LUDGVAN

Ludgvan has a very active Old Cornwall Society which has many fascinating archives and displays describing the history of the area.

The project has spoken to a dozen people who have talked about Ludgvan or 'Lugon' as they say!

Stretching from the coast to the heights of Castle Gate the parish seems to contain three distinct areas – the coast with its agricultural support industries at Long Rock, basket making and the Moon family, the hinterland, Crowlas and the Lower Quarter with its shops, 'stamps' and stories of children playing cricket in the main road early in the last century, and then Church Town, the ancient Church and its surrounding cottages. Between the two is the old school which provided our subjects with many happy memories, and the Vellanoweth valley.

We have been told wonderful stories of the farms and the crops, the dairy and the pubs. The Chapel at Crowlas provided much of the social activity of the area with its Sunday School Treats, Choir and visiting concert parties. There was the traditional Lower Quarter fair which has been described as a very important event with 'travellers' spending time in the village, horse sales, stalls and great fun for everyone!

One striking feature of this parish was the remoteness of some of the parts of the community and the lack of what today we would describe as utilities in many cottages until well into the middle of the 20th Century. Lack of mains electricity meant the use of 'flat irons' heated on the stove, listening to the radio powered by the 'accumulator' charged up by the local garage, lamps fuelled by paraffin delivered to the door, milked fetched directly from the nearest farm and the daily collection of water from the 'chute'. We usually associate the Cornish Range or slab, the boiler providing water for the Monday wash and bathing in front of the fire with the 1920's and 1930's but were clearly still part of many peoples daily routine even while Elvis was starting his career and TV was slowly spreading across West Penwith.

The Parish of Ludgvan

The history of Ludgvan goes back to Celtic times with the coming of the Irish Saint LUDWAN. Though this name has been changed many times to the present LUDGVAN. The church is now dedicated to St Paul.

This lovely area is pampered by the Gulf Stream which makes it very similar to the Mediterranean climate and encourages early growth for various crops. Many people were employed on the land as labour was all manual.

I can remember the times when life was less hectic than today and we were contented with our lot.

The sweet smell of soil being ploughed, the dew on a summer's evening. The sweet sound of various birds at dawn. How good it was to see the mist rise from the land after warm rain.

Although we worked hard we also had our leisure times. The Church and Chapel both had good congregations and were well supported. Besides the usual services there were always concerts and other forms of entertainment organised, when almost all the villagers would take part one way or another. Of course, most activities involved music and there were many good voices to be heard on Sundays and often for the non-churchgoers the local pubs where someone would strike a chord and others join in. It was mostly the farm workers who would sing over their well earned pint of beer! When the potato season came around there was always pleasant rivalry as to which 'boss' had grown the biggest potato!

The flower season provided plenty of work for the women. They needed the money to provide extras for the home, especially at Christmas and school clothes.

The Women's Institute was well supported and was a welcome break from the hard graft. Several young women organised a Young Wives group and were always holding fund raising efforts for charities. I remember we once made enough to buy each pensioner a half hundred weight of coal which was about 2/6d!

Carol Singing was another money raiser. About 20 or so enjoyed this annual event. This was when the husbands would join the wives. We used to go around the Parish, to the farms where we often had a small glass of sherry. Hence we got home with rather rosy cheeks! I remember when we reached Ludgvan Rectory to sing to Canon and Mrs Murley she always gave us a sweet. Then we all trouped into the White Hart where the landlord would serve some food. Down Church Hill to Crowlas. There was always such a good feeling of goodwill and companionship; all were willing to help out in time of need. I also remember when a farmer was attacked by a bull and almost died. All the neighbours took turns to look after his livestock as well as their own until he recovered. Sadly he never fully recovered.

In 1963 there was foot and mouth out break not far from us but thankfully we were not affected. We took all precautions and escaped the disease.

Today when I look out across the Bay and watch the sea changing every day, St Michaels's Mount and to Mousehole and Newlyn, nothing has changed- only people and their lifestyle. I wonder if it is better, I doubt it. Where is the community spirit? With so many incomers our identity is sadly disappearing. But then, the whole world is changing too.

Never make the mistake of calling Marazion a village – you will soon be told ...it's a town

MARAZION

We have been given many such images as this which evoke memories of times past and old friends

We have recorded lots of memories of the School, its teachers and the changes in the buildings. Before the present school the boys and girls were taught separately in the town and Mr. Round, the head who really established the new school was a remarkable man. We have recorded fond and some not so fond memories!

There have been and still are lots of great characters in the town and we have met many fine story tellers!

Traditions and continuity are important to the people of Marazion. Whether 'born & bred' or newly arrived, all are assimilated into a strong community.

We have many memories of the war with Americans billeted, the beach mined, defensive guns on the Mount and children growing up intrigued by events. One subject who was a teenager in the war was asked for their reminiscences – I can't remember anything, they said, I was just having a good time! There were common memories such as the Messerschmitt displayed in the square or the machine gun attack on town, the effect of the Land Army girls and rationing.

The Mount plays an important role in the town and we have recordings of people who grew up on the island with all its benefits, including missing school.

Marazion had a village bobby, notably PC Allen who handed out his own fair justice.

In the first half of the 20th Century Marazion had over 30 shops, fulfilling all the needs of the populous – many regretted that it was now very different.

Groups, charities, the Church & Chapel, the Institute and the Pubs and Hotels all provide a background to community life – many raising thousands for charity.

The station was also important, not only providing for many travellers to and from the Town but also sending produce to market – people often grew a few flowers in their gardens and sold them in London. The 'bus service was a vital life line too.

Visitors have always come to Marazion but our subjects have made sure that we understand that Marazion is much more than a beach with a view of the Mount.

In correspondence with Francis Richards, T.R. (Roy) Jewell remembers some of the characters from his youth:

I remember sitting at the back of the Chapel listening to Rev Highfield with his shock of white hair. He was known to us as Padereski. One day he was attacked at the door of the Manse by two robbers. He fought them off and according to the press brought one down with a rugby tackle- well he was a Rugger 'blue'.

Miss Richards – a great worker for the overseas missions lived next to the Chemists.

My favourite Sunday school teacher was Mr. Calf, the newsagent. He took Bible Class and we always asked him about his experiences as a ships carpenter and going around the Horn. He would entertain us for a while but always came back to religion by warning us of the dangers facing young men in foreign ports. I do not think any of that class –Francis and Arthur Hosken, Roy White, Arnold Williams, Clarry Pearce, Dick Laity and I (the youngest) went further than St Michael's Mount!

My uncle Jack was the Wheelwright at Shop Hill had an iron trough shaped like a wheel outside the shop on waste ground. He would place a wheel in the trough and fill it with water. The blacksmith would then bring out the red hot iron band and shrink it on the wheel.

Billy Baker pumped the Chapel organ but sometimes fell asleep and Arthur Phillips would have to go behind and wake him up. Many of us took a turn at the pump if Billy was ill.

Two Miss Pearces sold sweets, biscuits from those large square tins, a few groceries and vinegar from a barrel. I used to like fetching this in a jug and sipping it on the way back. Mother used this to marinade pilchards which were plentiful.

George Hill who went around lighting the oil street lamps.

My father was a tailor and outfitter with a good business with 12 staff but when Burtons and the 50 shilling Tailor came to Penzance he could not compete.

Theophilus Care lived in a cottage behind Tom Reynolds Butchers Shop. He was a jobbing mason and carried everything on a ladies bicycle which he sometime rode! He always wore a school cap and had a clay pipe in his mouth and kept a punt below the cliff. Boys were always taking it to sea but always brought it back. He got fed up and took the bung out. Ernie Williams and I did not know this and after Sunday school pushed it off only to find water pouring in. We got back but our blue serge suits were white with salt.

On the occasion of the visit of Prince Chichibu, a Japanese who was being entertained at the Castle by Brigadier Lord St Levan a red carpet was laid between the Goldolphin steps and Chapel Rock. The Flemington brothers and a Police Inspector escorted the Prince to the waiting barges with the crews in their special; uniforms.

The Flemington's were the St Levan family chauffeurs. Father had the contract to supply their uniforms, the Butlers and two footmen and the boatmen's nearly every year together with the gamekeeper's breeches and Holmes, the head gardener a bowler hat!

Jim Mudge, whose only gainful employment was shrimping.The summers always, seemed warm and he would wear a light weight khaki suit with the legs rolled up plus plimsolls. He could find shrimps where we failed and after cooking would carry then in punnets on a large tray around his regulars for a few pence a punnet.

THE PROJECT CREATED 85 RECORDINGS OF ARCHIVE QUALITY.

The following are examples of the personal stories we have preserved

MARAZION MEMORIES

John Allen

John Allen's father was the Policeman in Marazion from 1939 to 1953. John grew up in the town and later pursued his own very successful career in the Police but his father had a tremendous impact on the community – he was very much 'the village bobby'. He was born on Christmas Day 1903 in Truro where his father was a Park keeper. He joined the Cornwall Constabulary in 1923.

John told us many stories about his father's time in the town:

He had been stationed at Falmouth, Newquay, Saltash, Perranporth and Sennen before moving to Marazion in September 1939. Police cover was fairly sparse, there were other Policemen at St Hilary, Crowlas and they were under the supervision of a Sergeant at Penzance – their only vehicle was a bicycle but each Police House did have the phone!. Arthur Allen was always on duty –

John on duty in 1990

"*If people came to report anything they would come to our front door and you can imagine that whilst we were all sitting huddled around the stove listening to the radio in the dinning room, father would say – everybody out, this is the interview room!*"

Arthur Allen middle row, second from the right

John remembers that his father always had his police trousers on so that he was ready for duty whether gardening, fishing or decorating! The Police Station became the centre of activity being the Police Station as well as the family home! PC Allen was legendary for knowing everything and everyone! His own brand of justice dealt with many minor infringements of the law and in fact there was very little crime. Each day his father would receive the Police Gazzette with the latest on crime and criminals and he had to update his paperwork – a task he never relished in fact he would call it the 'guts ache'.

When his father retired he became chauffeur to Lady St Leven which enabled him to stay in the town. His 14 years stationed in one place was very unusual but underlines the affection felt between policeman and Town.

" The nearest sergeant was at Penzance operating from Eastern Green we were County policemen rather than Town. His duties were based around the principle of waking or riding your bike but father had the gift of being able to stand outside the front door and always getting a lift! Father knew everyone and everyone knew father."

"One day Father and the Sergeant brought a fellow in for stealing wire from the allotments. He was not admitting it and Father wanted to go back up to the allotment to get further evidence. In those days the collecting of evidence such a foot prints was very new but father was interested in this aspect of the work and eventually he solved the case by taking a plaster cast of a footprint!. So they did not quite know what to do with the suspect while they returned to the scene of the crime. John was 15 and the sergeant told the much larger suspect to sit in the chair and await their return or the young boy would sort him out! To John's amazement he did."

John and Anne Allen in their garden in Ludgvan

PEOPLE - JOHN ALLEN

Peter Badcock

Peter and friend!

Born into a farming family in 1928 at Middle Colenso Farm, Peter remained a farmer all his life. His father came from Lamorna, his mother Goldsithney and after serving in the Ist World War his father returned to the farm, taking on Trevarthian Farm, part of the St Aubyn Estate in 1934.

Peter was a young man during the War, leaving school to work on the farm. He remembers as a child taking care of the two 'home' cows – kept for the milk to drink and make butter and cream and war being declared on the wireless- run by accumulator batteries. 'It was only Father who decided what we would listen to – nobody else had a choice!'

They had 7 Land Girls on the Farm – it was very labour intensive with lots of hand and shovel work – they also had 7 men and grew about 60 acres of broccoli, 10 acres of sugar beet as required by the government, 40 acres of corn plus the cattle. Peter remembers that they bought South Devons from Spring Fairs in Devon which would come by rail arriving at Mara Zion Station and then they would drive the cattle up through Marazion – three men and a dog to move 60 head of cattle! The Land Army girls needed a lot on instruction and showing what to do but many stayed and married local men. Many farm labourers were not allowed to go to war (reserved occupation) but had to serve many hours in the Home Guard. Peter says that this involved long hours – in the summer months there was double summer time so at very busy times such as hay harvest they could be working in the fields as late as 11.pm and then have to go on watch in pill boxes around the coast,. However they still had to be back at work by 7.30 next morning.

Peter's father was a local councillor and he remembers him, telling the family what he had done over the tea table. Peter followed his example and served for over 40 years.

Farmers in Marazion always took sea weed from the beach and Peter says there were always lots more horses on the farms around the Town rather than in-land. You always saw horses or tractors on the beach. Sea weed and sand were 'lugged' from the shore and put in piles on the farm, other matter was added including offal and this would be turned twice during the winter, by fork, to rot down and then spreading on the land to build up the soil. This is done much less these days – it was very hard work and today's seaweed is full of plastic and other non biodegradable detritus.

Having known the St Aubyn Estate for many years Peter has seen many changes. The rent court continues. When we recorded Peter in 2005 he had just attended that year's – beef and vegetables from local suppliers with over 65 attendees. The idea of the court was to pay the rent. Peter remembered that his father took over their farm at a time when farming was unprofitable and was able to insist that the Estate established a water supply through out the farm before he took over the tenancy and he paid an annual rent of one pound an acre for the 316 acres farm. There were four pheasant woods on the farm and during the war there was no pheasant rearing so the trees were felled for uses such as pit props leaving the outer edge so the area was intact for later.

Peter and Greta outside their farmhouse

A modern day harvest? Photo: Yvonne Oates

Roy and Muriel Badcock

Both Mr and Mrs Badcock come from farming families.

Roy's family moving through a series of tenancies to build their business and always supplementing their crop growing activities by taking in visitors.

His mother was an excellent cook – even the Doctor would make a weekly visit for some of her home cooking!

Mr Badcock succeeded his father as in turn his sons have taken on the farm from him. He went from school straight to the business and remembers the particular pressures during the War. They used Land Girls at busy times such as potato picking and also used Italian and later German prisoners of war as labourers. He remembers the Germans being the better workers. What they could grow was controlled by 'WARAG' so that the county quotas could be fulfilled. Crops were taken by rail – he remembers once by boat – and Marazion Station was a very busy place with farmers queuing to unload heir produce. Transferring Sugar Beet could take all day and they had special forks designed to move the beet easily. They did not know where it went – it was sold to local agents. As well as the usual crops, Mrs Badcock's family grew flowers but this stopped during the war as trains would not take them – some small producers took flowers to market in suitcases to get over the ban. Tractors became more widely available and the Badcock's also had a lorry. They only used this once to move seaweed from the beach but it was not a very happy experience as they got stuck in the sand and the sea water was very corrosive –"More trouble than it was worth". Mrs Badcock remembered the possie piles in Ludgvan – huge mounds of sea weed and 'lug sand' (sand taken from Marazion beach), left to rot before being spread on the land and with a terrible smell. The farmers were essential to the war effort but also participated in other ways – Mr Badcock was a member of Marazion Home Guard and remembers the nightly patrols and training every Sunday. Mrs Badcock's father was the ARP warden and would summon his colleagues by blowing an old Boer War Bugle. (The Bugle is still in the family!)

Mrs Badcock grew up in Ludgvan, her father farming near Castle an Dinas. They had two evacuees – two boys at the start of the war who returned home when the expected bombing did not materialise and later girls with whom she still keeps in contact. Mrs Badcock went to Lugdvan School and then West Cornwall in Penzance which was very strict. She remembers having to wear a hat, gloves and long stockings all year round and the girls were banned from walking down Causeway Head. She remembers lessons in York House and Chapel Street and then the building of the new part of the school – now the District Council Offices.

"My father lived until he was 91 but he ate so much cream that dieticians today said he should have been dead years before."

Causewayhead, 2009. Photo: Yvonne Oates

PEOPLE - ROY & MURIEL BADCOCK

Howard Curnow

Howard standing at Top Tieb, Marazion 1997

The Curnows came to St Hilary from Marazion in the 1860's. Howard's Great Grandfather had gone to Australia, made money, returned and invested it in land. He married and had 8 children. Howard's parents moved into the farm house in 1932 and did extensive renovations, especially to the kitchen.

> *There was an attic where an old aunt lived – when she died her mattress was put on the dung heap and as it disintegrated, revealed a number of gold sovereigns sewn into the mattress.*

Although only born in 1936, Howard has some memories of the war. He has a recollection of watching planes have a dog fight high in the sky over the village and a clear memory of the night when two bombs fell on Perran Downs. He was woken by the house shaking and comforted by his mother. Next day he and his brothers were taken by their father to look at the bomb craters!

There were a number of evacuees in the area, several billeted at St Hilary vicarage. Howard told the story of one young girl who came to the village with her two brothers:

"Evacuees were piled into a village hall like so many heads of broccoli or boxes of fish and the locals would come in and say – I'll have that one! In this case the girl and her two brothers had been told by their mother to stay together but no one could take on three children so they were left to the end and had to be split up. The two boys were together but a mile away from their sister. They were called Baatz and within a few months the little girl fell out of a tree and died. Her mother came down for the funeral but could not believe that her daughter had been evacuated to Cornwall for safety but had died. Her grave in St Hilary churchyard is inscribed 'evacuated with the angels'."

Howard began his schooling at St Hilary but soon moved to Marazion. He remembers travelling by Berrimans Bus which would stop in Goldsithney to wait for one of the boys to get out of bed! He joined the infant's class with Marjorie Floyd –'she was a typical little dumpy lady fussing around the children, then moved up into Miss Trevaskis' class – known as Louie Lollipop. He remembers being taught to swim by lying on a mat in the classroom! Next Miss Warren who always had a blazing fire and leaned against the brass rail around the fire. She was a very methodical teacher. Ambrose Richards took the top class and would always challenge you with a question when walking around the school: "7x8 boy?" Another memory was of getting the cane because he and Victor Oates had delayed returning to school from an errand into the Town by buying an ice cream. The punishment was immediate!

We also recorded his clear memories of the busy kitchen on the farm where ten sat around the table - 'when mother wasn't baking she had to be sleeping'.

The family had a nanny called Annie Floyd who lived-in and if she ever got fed up with the children misbehaving she would get the whitewash and paint the toilet down the garden, venting her anger on the walls. She and Howard's mother worked very hard, cooking for the men on the farm as well as her large family. Mother loved making cakes – seedy cake, saffron cake, heavy cake, sultana cake. Monday was wash day – Annie would light up the boiler early! The children were used as labour on the farm and at home. There was no water supply on the farm and they relied upon rain water which was collected in a huge tank. A dowser came once but only found water at a spot in a field where Howard's kitchen now stands. It was never drilled. Later they would collect water for the animals from the river at Relubbus or the adit at Trenow. Howard remembers the water jug being covered with a fine lace cloth which they also put over their glass to strain the water they drank – this would trap most of the dirt and grit and little red worms!

Beatrice, Howard and Florence Curnow Marazion School - 1947

George Curnow

George was born in 1934 at Lower Kenneggy, his father was a miner who worked in various mines in the district until he had to give up due to lung disease, from which time it was fishing which provided his income.

"During the war father was called up to the Devon and Cornwall Light Infantry but he was not fit enough and was sent to work as a Bevan Boy in East Pool Mine – he cycled there and back from Marazion everyday but it was too far so he got lodgings at Wall and we only saw him on Sundays."

George's father fished from Prussia Cove until the family moved to Marazion shortly before the Second World War. – the family came by road but Father and George came by boat!

"My father built a sailing work-boat at Prussia Cove and later converted it with an engine. At Prussia Cove there were little shacks which the fishermen used for generations. Father had one and he built one from Gunpowder Boxes – it lasted for many years. We used to go down on a Sunday when the men had lots of Spider Crabs and they would have a good old boil up and feed down on the cliff top. We used a boiler and fire for tarring the bottoms of boats as well."

George left school in 1949 – one of the first to stay on until 15. he remembered making many friends at school, Miss Floyd – lovely teacher- and playing football and cricket. We boys had gardening lessons and we would grow food for the canteen. George played football for Marazion - making his football debut aged 13! He remembers many distinguished Marazion players such as Jimmy Powell, Terry Scanlon, Walter Jago, Dick Hall, Ernie Martin Roy Stevens Jimmy Rodda Frank Blissett and Sid Trembath. His Mum had 6 children to care for – they kept Chickens in the garden and his mother would also salt down fish – drying it in the sun on a wire mesh with Rock Salt. There were no fridges in his youth -we had a safe outside so anything fresh would be put out there'.

Boats were always important to George. He worked with his father and also 'hobbled' from the Mount. Father made his own crab pots, withy was cut from Truthwall (Sam Collins farm) for the main structure and Tamarisk from the cliff tops made the base. They would 'lay' the trees when possible to make them grow straight and it also made a good hedge for the farmers.

George has maintained the tradition of picking Limpets and winkles from the beach. This used to be a great Good Friday tradition all around the coast. The French would come and pick winkles but not so many people do it now.

Another of George's memories was the Blacksmith and Wheelwright in Shop Hill:

" I remember Willie Trevaskis and Gerald Ivey, his apprentice, during the war. Mr John Jewell had a workshop there as well – he was a wheelwright and they used to work together. Mr Jewell would make the

PEOPLE - GEORGE CURNOW

wheel and Willie the metal band. I remember seeing them go across the road – they had a big metal rack and would stretch the white hot band over the wheel. It was an art and we would sit by watching"

Another memory was the liming of the Mount Causeway to destroy the weed at least once a year. They spread lime and sand over the roadway which killed the weed and filled the cracks in the stones. Nowadays they use acid which kills the weed but tends to lift the stones! The old system worked!!

George also worked for T F Hosking and enjoyed his association with the local farming community. He and his family emigrated to Australia in 1965 but North Queensland, where they lived suffered a drought, conditions were difficult and they returned home. It was only when he got back that George discovered he had relatives 'Down Under.'

"As a boy I lived next door to the Fire Engine Pub and sometimes, in the blackout, the American troops would emerge and fall over the wall into the gully next to our house! Mother would take them in, sort them out and send them on their way."

Photo: Yvonne Oates

PEOPLE - GEORGE CURNOW

Arnold Derrington

Arnold in 1945

Arnold was not born in Marazion and only lived there for a short period but his memories of the place are deep, clear and very important to him. Born in Devon in 1922, his father brought the family to St Erth when Arnold was 18 months old and thence to Marazion in 1930.

Arnolds memories of his youth in Marazion are amazing – characters like Mr. Round, the Head Teacher of Marazion School, Dr. Penny and his son Comet, Mr. Rundle who ran the Men's Institute, Ermantrude Harris and the Misses Gibson are all part of Arnold's reminiscences. A typical example is Jack Mudge the Shrimper who lived with his sister next to Parkins Shop and went out to the beach at low tide with his shrimp net over his shoulder and then sold his catch around the Town.

Arnold's school days and his school friends are very important. He remembers the daily routine at Marazion, his father paid £3- 5s a term to send him to Penzance Grammar School and the Empire Day Parade when Miss Hilaria St Aubyn presented copper coloured medals to the school children who then sang patriotic songs!

Mr. Philip Calf and Mr Sam Bamber were the Sunday School Superintendents:

Marazion Station, 2009.

Photo: Yvonne Oates

"Sunday School was a very happy place. We had outings at Semmons Picnic Grounds and also went on the train to Carbis Bay. We would all walk down to Marazion Station and take the train from there (Tea Treat).

Sometimes we would go on busses like Marazion Busses or Berrimans and we liked the drivers, especially Joe James who was later out milkman, because they were a very friendly lot!! We spent most of the day there – our parents went too and we went to St Ives shopping – very special. Paynes Picnic Grounds, swings, a big room where we could all eat a meal, of course there was a beach at Carbis Bay as well as a pond with boats on – tuppence or something to row a boat of your own!"

Arnold had a distinguished war career and is still in touch with the other two living members of his air crew of 7. He won the DFC. However his earliest experience of the 2nd World War was joining Marazion Home Guard:

"My father encouraged me to do so. We only had little caps to wear as a sign of a uniform – like a forage cap, and sometimes an arm band. We were known as the Local Defence Volunteers originally and I used to be on duty on Rodney Burrows out Virgin Hill way. I was on duty with Nicky Jenkin, Nicky Laity and Major Glass and because I was the youngest amongst the group I was the cyclist who was the runner to communicate between posts – there was no such thing as a mobile phone in those days. I think Clive Marriot, estate agent for Lord St Levan was in charge with Major Lister."

> KLISKIES:
> Arnold describes the making of little 'boats':
>
> *"We sailed boats in the lovely pool between Gwelva and Top Tieb. The Kliskie was made of a wild stalk with a feather. There was a rather bulbiferous thing called an Alexander and it had a hollow stem that would dry out very well. Indeed, if you got one with a curve in it wouldn't let the water in one end and that would be the bow of your boat. You would put in a feather as a sail and a little bit of slate as a keel and two feathers if you like set at 45 degrees, that would be a very nice thing to sail"*

Arnold at home in Pendeen - at 84 years

PEOPLE - ARNOLD DERRINGTON

Mary Brigid Greenwood Penny

No description of the community of Marazion could be complete without some mention of the Greenwood-Penny family. Mary Brigid, the widow of Dr Comet Greenwood-Penny comes from the Nottinghamshire/Derbyshire border where she was born into a medical family in 1933. She trained as a nurse at St. Mary's Paddington and worked in France before settling in Marazion in 1958.

> *"The predominant memory of my first impression of Marazion is the feeling of it – a feeling I still have – this is a special place. No one is ever apologetic about living in Marazion."*

The Greenwood–Penny family came to Marazion in the early 20th Century when Dr Sidney took up the practice of Dr Kenneth Bennetts. He had three children, the second of whom was Mary-Brigid's late husband Sidney Augustus who was always known as Comet because his father saw one through the window when his son was born! It is an unusual name and there are only 11 people in the whole world called Greenwood Penny today. Comet succeeded his father as the Marazion Doctor and has two sons, Robert and Julian.

Mary Brigid described the origins of the Greenwood Penny Christmas Fund which began in 1938. The Penny's were great carnival builders and at Christmas Dr. Sidney decided to convert a flat bottomed boat into a sleigh. He dressed as Father Christmas, his sons were Reindeers and on Christmas Eve they drove the sleigh down Causeway Head and Market Jew Street throwing sweets to the children. It was a great success and the following year they did it in Marazion. The event stopped for the war but resumed in 1946 and has taken place every Christmas Eve since, with a present being distributed to every child under the age of eight. A group raises funds throughout the year and the organisation was named in honour of Comet Greenwood Penny after his death in 1961. Both his sons carry on the tradition by serving on the committee.

Mary-Brigid gave us an insight into the life of a Doctor in the 1950's. The surgery in Marazion was at the side of the house and comprised of a waiting room, two consulting rooms and an office supervised my Mrs Peggy Kott. The dispensary was also at the surgery because if you lived outside the Town you could collect your medicines from the surgery but if you lived in the Town you had to use the Chemist! Getting to the Doctor was more difficult in those days because few people had cars so there were more home visits and Mary Brigid remembers driving her husband to many isolated places in the dark during his 'rounds'. The doctors were always on call and often had to go out in the middle of the night.

The surgery had two telephone numbers – one personal, the other for patients and when the phone was first put it the number was simply 5. There were no appointments and there were branch surgeries at Crowlas, Germoe and for a while at Ashton. These were weekly and held in a private house. Emergency cases also came to the surgery – cuts, accidents and minor surgery was all dealt with there.

The local Doctors and Vets had an annual dinner and worked closely together and there was some overlap in their dealings with the farming community!

Mary-Brigid herself was a nurse. Training in her day was very much an apprentice system-a few weeks instruction, an exam and then onto the wards, changing every three months. The ward sister completed your record book and there were exams at the end of each year. It was a four year professional training. It is very different now because of so many technological changes and stays in hospital are so much shorter. She remembers the first hip replacement, the hips were ceramic and they called them Pot Hips and when the patient first left the bed they were very worried in case the hip cracked!

Mary Brigid has always been interested in the theatre and when her family had grown up she became involved in local productions. She had a friend called Averil Cockbain who had been an actress and wrote, directed and made costumes for productions, especially for an organisation called the Cornwall Religious Drama Federation and the Minack Theatre.

Averil established Cape Cornwall Costumes in St. Just and Mary-Brigid became her successor in 1981 moving over 750 costumes into a building next to her house which she named 'The Wardrobe'. She ran the business for nearly 21 years and had more than 2,500 costumes when she finished. Mary Brigid enjoyed it greatly and met many very interesting people but maintaining all the clothes was an endless task! Her current interests are helping to make street banners, large pictorial flags and walking and caring for 'our amazing network of local footpaths.'

Below: Mary Brigid and Comet sailing their Redwing and right at the Hunt Ball in 1959

John and Molly Jago

Molly has a treasure trove of cuttings and photos describing past events of Goldsithney but John was born there in 1938 and described for us what it was like as he grew up.

He went to the Goldsithney School in South Road, although in his day there were less than 20 pupils. He has a memory of Miss Edmonds the teacher, but only that she wore her hair tied back in a small bun! From Goldsithney, he attended a small school in North Street, Marazion run by Miss Nash, where there were only 8 or 10 pupils! After a spell at St Erbyns, he attended Penzance Grammar School where he gained 5 'O' Levels, then a year working on a farm before going to Seale Hayne Agricultural College.

He has fond memories of National Service as part of the Intelligence Corps serving in the Army Headquarters in Germany (a building with 3 miles of corridors), during the Cold War. His department was responsible for much of the correspondence surrounding the capture of Gary Powers, the American U2 pilot by the Russians. He is also proud to claim he was in Berlin before the wall was built! Upon demob in 1960 he returned to Goldsithney and his uncle,s haulage firm, diversifying later into a building company - the firm he is still involved with today.

His memories of the village include the old blacksmith's shop - a regular meeting place for the men of the village. He remembers John Trevaskis, his brother Sam and his father pumping the bellows. There would be a happy crowd including 'Charlie Bob', Joe Perfect, Mr Hansen, Mr Curnow and Mr George Fox from the Post Office shouting the Test Match cricket scores to them.

There were several shops in the village; Miss Jordan's sweet shop, the middle shop run by Victor Beard and the very top shop, Arthur Hosken's. The Post Office doubled as a newspaper shop and was a busy place run by George Fox and later by his wife.

> *John also remembers buying 5 Woodbines from Mr Fanshaw's shop at the bottom of the village. These would be split from a packet of 10 and wrapped in newspaper.*

The garage next to the Post Office was run by Dickie Basher who had a little Austin 7, registration CV2719. He would push his cap to the back of his head if he had a problem, to reveal a very white forehead) Dick Vellanoweth had a carpenter's shop in the village and he made coffins as well.

The village was quiet with so little traffic that the boys would play cricket in Primrose Hill. There were both cricket and football teams and during the war, a fire engine was kept next to the Trevelyan Arms, a volunteer ambulance and crew at North Road and of course, a policeman.

As a boy, John remembers the sewage pipes being laid down the main street by Hunt's and he thinks the water pipes were put in by John Bennetts of Marazion. There was a water supply from a well at the top of the village and this pumped up to flow by gravity, down through the village with 6 or 7 stand pipes where water could be drawn.

Molly has also been very involved in village life, including fundraising to build and maintain St Piran's Hall and will be remembered for her famous cake stall on Charter Fair day, raising more than £10,000 over the years. A former chairman of the Village Hall Committee, she has been a big supporter of the Horticultural Show, Past Chairman of the Former Goldsithney Young Wives and Chairman of the PTA at St Hilary School. Whilst John has served as a Parish Councillor and District Councillor and becoming Chairman of the District 1989-1991. Incidentally, his grandfather was the first Chairman of the Parish Council. John Laity was also a member of the West Penwith Board of Guardians, which later became West Penwith District Council, in which he also served after it's formation.

Both John and Molly lament the lack of volunteers these days; the young don't seem to have the time. John is also a firm believer that the villages in Penwith have missed out in terms of resources and facilities compared to the larger towns in the area.

Sid Hayes

Sid was born in 1920, brought up in Plain-an-Gwarry, moving to St Hilary Church town when he was 12.

> *"Our first cottage had no water, sanitation or electricity. Nothing down Plain-an-Gwarry, even the roads were rough. We got our water from the well on the neighbouring farm."*

Our recording focused upon three areas of Sid's life:

THE CHURCH.

Sid always attended St Hilary Church walking there from Plain-an-Gwarry three times every Sunday. Sid remembers singing on the way home and believes that the weather was better in his youth. He sang in the Church Choir and took part in the Bethlehem Play that was broadcast. His claim to fame is that he appeared in the original production and the later one broadcast on the BBC in the 1990's. The first time he was the shepherd boy and last time the main shepherd, a part played by Nick Peters in the first production. He remembers the early broadcasts which were set up by Finson Young, a friend of the rector Bernard Walke. The church was a mass of wires and batteries and the voices were carried by landlines across the field and thence to London where the play was recorded on large 12inch discs – Father Walke had a copy of these. Sid's view of Bernard Walke was very positive - he did not appeal to everybody but I found him helpful in every way.

Photo: Yvonne Oates

THE ARMY.

Sid first worked on Kestle Farm and then for Mr. Bettens at Peranuthnoe. He remembers buying a brand new push bike for £7 – 10s, a huge amount in those days. He was a member of the Territorial Army based at Chy an Dour, Penzance and at the out break of war was called up, joining the Duke of Cornwall Light Infantry. His first posting was St. Just and then India! He saw much of the sub continent during his service – first at Lahore and then he was transferred to the Police taking charge of Italian prisoners with the help of Indian Units. He learned to drive on Salt Flats while based in Karachi and later spent time in Calcutta and Bombay. As the war progressed he was returned to the army for service in Burma, fighting in the jungle "swamps, mosquitos – terrible". On leaving Burma he had to march across the mountains to Calcutta and then transported to Bombay he sailed home. Sid also served in Europe, finally based near Hanover and ended his service in the 1950's in the Suez Canal Zone. He is justly proud of his service, medals and continuing association with the Burma Star Organisation.

ENTERTAINMENT.

Sid recorded his memories of going to Penzance for an evening's fun. Berriman's 'bus only cost a penny or two pence. He remembers going to Corpus Christie Fair with only sixpence to cover his fare and the evening out – it was a huge fair with lots to do even if you could not afford the rides. The last bus home was always an event – Joe Berriman always has 'room for one more'

"If you did not get the 'bus you had to walk home! Of course we also went by bike and would leave the cycle in an alley way with no lock or anything and when we came out of the cinema it was always still there! You could sit in the balcony of the Regal for 1/3d but we sat on the sides for nine pence. We used to love the Cowboy films"

Sid answering questions at St Hilary school

PEOPLE - SID HAYES

Gill Joyce

Gill's parents had arrived at the Mount in 1930 to work in service for the St. Aubyn family, Dad from Suffolk as a footman/valet and Mum from Newcastle as a parlour maid. They married in secret in 1932 (servants were not allowed to marry) and moved to work in Berwickshire in 1935. They returned to Marazion in 1947 when Mr Ager was appointed as Butler to the 3rd Lord St Levan. Gill was 11.

> "I was amazed when I first saw St. Michael's Mount – to live on an island in the middle of the ocean!!.

- Growing up on the Island was great fun. There were many established families who lived there and all worked for the family or the estate. They swam in the harbour, enjoyed an active outdoor life and pretty much had free reign of the island but could not play where they could be seen by anyone from the family.

- Butler Ager had a strict routine. He cleaned his own family's shoes each morning before going up to the castle – he could do the climb in 4.5 minutes. He would wake his Lordship, supervise the study, clean the silver, receive daily instructions from Lady St. Levan, serve light lunch for the family and then return home for the afternoon, often tending his own garden. Back to the castle about 5.30 pm.to supervise Dinner which was always formal for his Lordship and thence home for his own supper at 9.p.m

- Stanley Ager had a fantastic career – from boot boy in a London Hotel to Butler in Cornwall. He was always totally discreet about the families for whom he worked but was once featured in TV programme by Robert Robinson and helped write a book[†] on the skills of the Butler. The Butler's pantry was an important place and there was a clear hierarchy between the domestic staff.

- Going to school for the Island children was great fun – in bad weather they would arrive at school soaked to the skin. Gill remembers the smell of coats and shoes drying out by the fire. If the weather turned they would sometimes have to go home early and Gill had friends on the mainland that she could stay with if she could not get across.

Gill and her parents and children on the castle steps.

- In the 1930's and 1940's the life of the Lord St Levan was very grand. Lots of travelling with many trunks and of course great respect – servants never contradicted, even if they knew his Lordship was wrong. If you met a member of the family in the corridor the servant would stand still until they had passed and only spoke if spoken to first.

- Gill's father always described himself as a servant and believed that good service should always be tipped! He was himself a generous tipper.

- Gills affinity and affection for the Mount is long lasting. Both her parents are buried on the Mount, she herself was married on the Mount in 1958 (only the third marriage there that century) as was her daughter in 1990!

I had to get used to the expressions to do with the sea, the state of the tide the different landing stages at different states of the tide. We had to catch the duty boat at 8 o'clock to get to school – there were not so many hobblers* in those days – and we took the post boat at 4.30 to get home. The post boat would always go at 4.30 – whatever the state of the sea. John the postman always said 'nothing stops the Royal Mail'!"

* Mount ferrymen.

† *The Butler's Guide to Clothes Care, Managing the Table, Running the Home and other Graces* by Stanley Ager and Fiona St. Aubyn - published by Simon and Schuster
and *Ager's Way to Easy Elegance* by Stanley Ager - published by Bobbs-Merrill

Photo: Yvonne Oates

Myra Kitchen

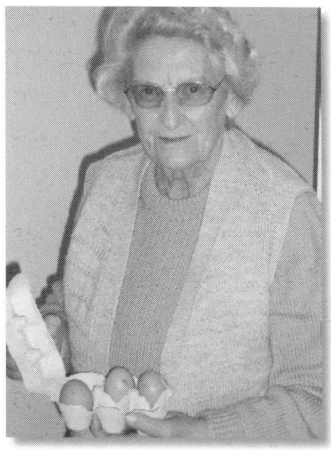

Myra was born in Goldsithney in 1922 and lived there all her life. Her memory of the village and how it changed is encyclopaedic and her recording is full of information about times past. Her mother died when she was very young and her father, a post man brought her and her siblings up in a small cottage in the village. Her husband came from Tresoe and worked in the tin streams by Wheal Gilbert. Her husband, son and grandsons all played Cricket for Goldsithney and the club has played an important part in her social life!.

"We spent every Saturday watching cricket"

- The cottage where Myra was brought up had no running water or electricity, neither did her first marital home. She did not have electricity at home until 1956 and the only running water was from the Keeve which collected the rain water from the roof. Myra described the sanitary provision of her childhood home as 'Bucket and Chuck it!'

- As a child she would fetch water from the village chute and milk from the nearest farm – straight from the cow to the table John Andrewartha was the farmer and he treated his cows like children – well cared for. His wife ran the dairy and was known as John Sharp and Polly Blunt!

- She remembers as a child being told that Lady Townsend was due to travel through the village and went to sit on the step outside the shop waiting to see the great Lady. When she eventually arrived it turned out to be a 'bus! Along with many others she

Photo: Yvonne Oates

Perran Cross today. Photo: Yvonne Oates

talked of Berriman's Bus – Joe Berriman would collect your order for something special from Penzance, get it and deliver it on the way back!!

- The local youth 'promenaded' every Sunday from Perran Cross Roads to Rosudgeon. Others went to Penzance Promenade or on a Saturday to walk up and down the Terrace in Penzance but Myra and her friends met a Perran Cross Roads every Sunday after Chapel or Church. Young men came from the whole area to meet girls!

- Another social meeting place was Tea Treats. Held in every village, always with a Brass Band (Carleen and St Dennis – very special) it was a place for men to meet girls. Goldsithney Chapel Tea Treat was the 3rd Saturday in June. They would march through the village and the children always have new clothes and would carry walking sticks dressed with flowers.

- Myra remembers Cobham's Flying Circus coming to Crowlas (1935). She remembers walking down 'Long Lanes' with her friend Teresa Richards, carrying her picnic. Her husband to be, went up in a plane

- The Chapel provided entertainment in the village. She remembers a Magic lantern Show and concert parties like the Hayle Merrymakers with Laurie Quinn. St Hilary Feast Concert had a group called the Truro Butterflies, and Tommy Reynolds from Marazion ran a Concert Party which always poked fun at the village characters!

"I'll tell you what – we had the best years. No-one today is as happy as we were in those days. More contented, never had very much, never wanted much. Happy as kings. Never had toys – we made the best of Christmas with a Tree and things – we had books as presents but I never remember having a doll, not as a child. Always in your stocking was a book, a pack of play cards like Happy Families, an orange and an apple, a piece of coal and a penny for good luck"

PEOPLE - MYRA KITCHEN

Howard King

Howard wrote his own story:

I was born in Relubbus in November 1918. My father, Sam King was a butter and egg merchant and my mother was Honor Lemin, daughter of John Lemin, a miner who lost both his hands in an explosion at Tregurtha Mine in 1891, the year of the Great Blizzard.

He was taken to West Cornwall Infirmary and was kept warm by putting newspaper and brown paper around him! He survived and was fitted with artificial hands with which he became very proficient.

Stanhope Forbes, the celebrated Newlyn artist often painted at Relubbus. I stood for him holding a hoop. When he painted the village pump another boy got there before me and got the sixpence. He once painted Miss Alice Dale sitting in a basket chair and asked 100 pounds for it – she refused although she could well afford it as her estate eventually funded the Alms House 'Alldale' in Relubbus Lane. Relubbus was always prone to flooding making it difficult to tell the river from the road this once happened to a herd of cattle being driven through the village.

In my childhood in Relubbus everyone knew everyone. Life revolved around the school and the chapel. A few were Anglicans but in the main either Methodists or indifferent. Three services on a Sunday and class and prayer meetings in the week. Prayer meetings could go on a bit. And some would get carried away with their own eloquence! People in general had profound respect for the Sabbath, only the absolute necessary was done on the farm and many would not carry water from the well or the pump- that would be done on Saturday. One old miner who had a small holding would plough on a Saturday night with a hurricane lantern at each end of the meadow. His wife would come and call out the time so he could finish before the Sabbath.

As I grew older and started to show some interest in music and was taught by Miss Pearl Hosken, followed by Miss Grace Bonnet and Mr Francis Williams on the organ. Later I was skilled enough to set down two carols, unique to St Hilary Parish "let Christians all with one accord" and a setting of the popular carol "Hark What Music". These carols were kept alive by Mr. Eddie Varker who with a few others sang them around the parish at Christmas.

Come the war, which changed our world, the LVD (Home Guard) was a boost to morale although the officers in charge were still thinking Ist World War! Locally there were three platoons – Relubbus Lane under Lieut. S Littler, Groft Gotha - Lieut. J Laity and Perran let by Capt. White. Groft Gotha guard hut was manned by night and training was on Sunday morning on Halamanning Park with occasional field exercises. On one occasion a visiting officer of Boer War vintage had the whole platoon excavating a trench on the burrows with one entrance and no exit – a suicide bunker. Cecil Andrews faced the trench with Cornish hedging.

The women's land army, that grand band of girls coming from a totally different environment soon made their presence felt. Work on the farm was very much harder than today. Harvesters were unknown, Potatoes were planted and picked by hand –the same for broccoli and cabbage. It could be soul destroying, back breaking work. They also picked violets and anemones though that was not part of their duties. Flower growing , the backbone of our local economy suffered during the war owing to a lack of transport and there were stories of people travelling to London with suitcases full of flowers rather than clothes. I had two girls, one from London, the other from Wales and two better tempered harder working girls it would be difficult to find. Quite a few girls married Cornish boys and infused new blood into West Cornwall.

The Women's Land Army outside their hostel in St Hilary.

Photo: Yvonne Oates

Anne Laity

Anne Laity (nee Waller) was born in 1936 in Aldershot moving to Marazion just before she was 9 because of her poor health. Her parents knew people who had moved to the Town, came for a holiday and decided to move themselves. Anne's father was a printer and got work at first with Wardens in Marazion and then with Mitchell's in Hayle.

Anne today with the view from her home.

She attended Marazion School, then Penzance Grammar before training as a nurse in Exeter. Anne described teenage life in Marazion:

"We used to have good entertainments – a film show up at the Town hall every Saturday, we had dances in the Clipper Café, a youth club in the old Methodist School room. Of course we also got up to mischief – but all harmless fun. There was also the Church Drama Group and we children would all appear in their annual pantomimes. In the summer everyone would congregate to go on the beach or the Folly Field and play games in the evening – the whole community. There were tennis courts where the boat pound is now and of course the Carnivals were always wonderful – I was the Carnival Queens attendant one year."

Anne is very proud of the Caravan Site business she and her husband built from nothing –'literally mine waste' at Wheal Rodney. She married Rex in 1956, he worked for T.F. Hosken and they moved into a small bungalow on the site – she grew flowers in the meadows but had no water, no electricity, an earth closet toilet and they collected rain water and her father-in-law brought her a churn of drinking water everyday. They used Tilley light and a Tilley iron – paraffin driven which had to be pumped up with a mantle. They later bought a generator. The next step was to build a 'Cornish Unit' bungalow of their own (prefabricated concrete) with mains services. They bought the burrows from St Albyn Estate and having gained planning permission set up the camp site in 3 months – levelling and grassing the site, putting in a septic tank and building a toilet block. Today it has touring vans, residential units and 10 holiday bungalows, a leisure complex and a swimming pool.

Community is very important to Anne, as it was for Rex. He was a town councillor as a teenager and they served twice as the Mayor and Mayoress. Anne regrets that Marazion has changed so much. When she was a child everyone knew everyone else but no longer. She believes community spirit is diminishing. She also remembers some of the characters of her youth – Dolly Warden who was so short she had a raised platform behind the counter of her shop, Jimmy Culley – bent double but a lovely man and Barber Hocking who had a shop at the top of Leys Lane who got called home for dinner by his wife and would leave the customer mid haircut! There was also the 'sand man' who lived in Leys Lane and delivered sand with his Donkey for them to spread on their kitchen floors.

"I'm more Cornish than Hampshire, because of my love for Marazion."

Benny Lugg

Benny as a young man.

Mr. Lugg was born in 1932 at the old Coastguard Station Marazion – the birth was registered with Frederick Walford Hockin, acting registrar and town Barber – his shop was at the top of Leys Lane!! Benny left Marazion School at 14 and went to work for the St Aubyn Estate – he still does!

"When the war came along all the windows in the school had this net pasted on so that if there was a blast the glass would not fly everywhere. When we had raids we had to congregate in the school corridor, away from the windows and we would all sing songs until the 'all clear'. The School bell was not rung during the war, it was reserved for warning of invasion, so Mr. Round would sound a car horn instead! We had to carry a gas mask in a cardboard box which soon became tattered and we then buy a round tin and put in that but they would clatter about and the seal would get damaged. Periodically Mr. Tonkin, the ARP Warden used to come into school, inspect the masks and repair them. There were about 160 children in the school and the top class was divided by a curtain. When it was cold the huge Cornish Range would be lit and children who brought lunch could warm their pasties."

The war period was well remembered by Benny – his father was a farm labourer and a member of the Territorial Army so was called up and away for the whole war – He remembers the Royal Enniskillen Fusiliers billeted at the Chy Morvah, the old vicarage and the Godolphin Hotel. They moved out and others came in – eventually the 'yanks'. Of these he has memories of characters such as 'Smasher Louis' (he was a boxer) and the men playing a game throwing horse shoes at a stake. One memory was of a group of the boys being called in to sing to an american-italian soldier to cheer him up.

> *The Americans would buzz around the town in their jeeps – all of which had pet names such as Mickey Mouse.*

Benny and his family attended the Ebenezer Chapel. He remembers Sunday school outings by train to Carbis Bay where you could ride on a Donkey, marching behind the Marazion Town Band and visits Freddy Reynolds Picnic Grounds. He also was paid 7/6d a quarter to 'blow' the Chapel Organ. He remembers playing below the cliff face at Venton, known locally as 'Target' which was part of the rifle range across the beach. He would dig bullets from the cliff and the remains of the concrete base for the target can still be seen. Benny also reminisced about the New Town area of Marazion – old thatched cottages and Jimmy Lawrence running the camping grounds. The station was very important to the town with tons of produce being sent to market. Benny would sometimes use the train to get home from Penzance. The 'bus fair from the top of the town was 4d return whereas take the train and walk only cost 21/2d.

He joined the St Aubyn estate straight from school – as an apprentice carpenter on £1 a week. The building team was 2 carpenters, a mason and a labourer. They developed into Godolphin Company and did work outside the Estate. When not working in Marazion he would get 12/6 a quarter cycle allowance for getting to work! Since 1889 there had been a carpenter's shop with attached accommodation. The old carpenter had been Mr Bennett and his wife ran a dressmaking business from their cottage. He left in about 1920 to be followed by Bertie White and then in 1958 Benny moved in to the workshop and cottage.

The Estate also employed Game Keepers and woodsmen and they had a sawmill at Truthwall. Mr. Dickie Lanyon from Rospeath with his traction engine would be hired to come and drive saw for the large timbers. After the war the supply of wood was regulated and they needed a permit.

Benny celebrating his Golden wedding.

> *All workers received a Christmas bonus – he remembers 10/- but in earlier days it used to be paid in vouchers to avoid the men drinking the money away!*

They always worked on the Mount and when Benny became the foreman he also worked on other projects such as laying new cables, a water main and relaying the cobbles on the Island.

Throughout his career he has done work on the Mount – castle and harbour. Much had been done to the Church, the causeway had to be maintained and some of it re-laid. He described the 'closing rock' on the eastern edge just on the Island side of halfway. As the tide came in if you could see this rock you could wade across in thigh boots but once it was submerged you had to take to a boat. Different landings on the mainland side were used by the boatmen at different stages of the tide. The causeway was built by Johnny Uren and Cooks Landing part way across the causeway was named after his labourer, Howard Cook. He understands that at one time there was a school on the Island and 4 pubs! He also has vivid memories of the railway which carried goods up to the castle. According to Benny the original was very crude and running it was skilled – It would be wound to the top and released quickly to avoid jumping the tracks and the brake at the bottom had to be applied at just the right moment to prevent it jumping out into the harbour.

Herbert Phillips

Herbert was born in Venton View, Marazion in 1918 and has lived all his life in the area. His father played the organ in the Methodist Chapel and Herbert remembers:

"When I was a little boy he would take me up to the organ and I would sit there next to him and then he would point to a stop and I could pull it. Another little thing I used to do for a couple of shillings was helping the organ tuner by holding down the keys."

Herbert has shared some fabulous stories some of which appear on the CD. He recalls being a member of the Marazion Scout group – Francis Hosken was the group scout master, Arthur his brother was the Scout Master and Herbert was his assistant. The Scout Hall was the old school on the main street in Marazion. They did lots of activities including going to a huge Jamboree at Mount Edgecombe in Plymouth. During the war he was a member of the Home Guard, latterly at Perranuthnoe under Captain White. He remembers the fighter plane crashing into the Marsh and the Home Guard had to guard the scene, including the dead pilot, until it was removed the next day!

One of Herbert's many passions were Motor Bikes. As a youth he kept one in the Piggery at the farm and rode around the fields. Later he and his mates would go on longer trips – Exeter to watch speedway or to spend a Saturday in Plymouth. Saturday was of course a working day and he would persuade his father that he could do extra on Friday to get off early. No Tamar bridge they would catch the last Torpoint ferry home, eat in the Fish and Chip shop in Torpoint and then proceed westwards along deserted roads.

During his life time domestic arrangements have changed enormously. Electricity arrived after the war, before that they had 'Aladdin' and 'Tilly' lamps. His father installed a small gas holder with a tray of carbide in the bottom, drip water onto it and it would give off a gas which ran small lights in the kitchen but they took candles to bed. The 'slab' was of course the centre of the home and Herbert remembers drying himself off in front of the fire box after a wet morning in the fields.

Marazion fair was a big event and he remembers the Fire Engine Inn being very busy and rowdy during the Fair time. He has also been closely associated with the Sailing Club. He crewed on many boats and recorded information about 'Jolly Boats' built by Willie Matthews upon his return from South Africa.

Herbert tells a good story! He shared that of the Egg Inspector during the war on the Lizard. He would check with egg producers that none were being sold off the ration One old lady who often shared a few eggs with the locals was warned that this man was on the look out and sure enough he appeared at her gate asking if she had a few eggs to spare. He was somewhat surprised (but pleased) when she readily agreed and she produced a bag with the eggs! He thought he had caught a black marketeer until he open the bag to discover half a dozen china eggs!!

West Cornwall Scouts 1939.

Zena Row

Rosina Mary Brann was born in 1922 in Crowlas –

"Crowlas Town as we knew it. We had a boot and shoe maker, a tailor, a family called Rowe who made baskets including large mawns to be used in the fields.

Mr. Verran provided us with batteries and mended our bicycles. At the top of the village was a lady milliner and in Blowing House Hill there was a tailoress. The Star inn of course and two doors down Mrs Hammill was a dressmaker. A food shop was run by two ladies called Wimbledon and Miss Ninns also ran a shop and the present post office was a lovely grocery shop run by Freddy Curnow and his wife. The grocery shop at the cross roads was originally the old toll house."

> *Mrs Row provided us with vivid memories of the villages of Crowlas and Ludgvan. The first five years of her life were spent living on the main road and she remembers an old grey open topped bus called 'The Defender' went through every day.*

She also recalled the main road being tarmaced, they widened the road and took some of the garden from their cottage. She can only remember one car in the village but lots of wagons, jingles and when electricity was brought in it cost householders five pounds to bring it into the home. Zena's father was a postman based at the Long Rock sorting office and delivering as far as Nancledra. Crowlas was flooded in the 1920's and the piano was ruined, the carpets had to be thrown away and the pigs at the bottom of the garden had to stand on their hind legs hanging onto the fence to keep above the water level! When she was 5 the family moved to Church Hill.

Zena's schooling began at Ludgvan which she remembers as very flexible. The teachers were Mr. Reid, Mr Angwin, Lucy Trembath and Amy Jones. Zena was good at drawing and it was arranged that she could go to the Art School in Penzance on Saturdays. Hayle Grammar School came next – riding her bicycle every day in her Blazer and felt hat. There were about thirty girls in the school, taught by Edith Wagner whose father 'Boss' Wagner and Mr. Jones taught the boys. Shorthand typing was part of the curriculum with the girls walking to Mellanear for lessons. From school Zena went to work at the Education Office in Chapel Street Penzance with Mr Jackson and Miss Axworthy, dealing with the placement of evacuees.

Zena attended the Church but spent more time in Crowlas (Churchtown was more distinguished because it had the Rectory and the Hunt !) She remembers lots of activity in Lower quarter with the carpenter and the blacksmith and collecting water from the chute. As children they would watch wheels being made with the hot iron rim being cooled in the water from the chute.

There were Donkey races in the field and the annual Ludgvan Fair in October with pony sales in the Fairfield (where there are houses today) and stalls down the road which were lit up at night by means of Naptha . She remembers a Mr Darby – a traveller who was an artist and would paint Inn signs and the like and once was invited to the school to entertain the children. Concerts in Crowlas were splendid – held in the Sunday School. Concert parties would come to entertain – Tom Reynolds from Marazion and she clearly remembers Annie Guard who would imitate Charlie Chaplin.

Pauline & Alfred John Rowe

Mr. Rowe born 1922, Mrs Rowe 1926. Married 1950

In a long and very interesting interview with Jane Howells made in 2005, Mr and Mrs Rowe described their long and hard working lives. Today Pauline is a stalwart of the Ludgvan Old Cornwall Society but she was born in Camborne, her father a blacksmith with Holman Brothers. One of 5 children she describes her childhood as 'lovely' despite once having 'a ruler over her hand' for drawing an unflattering picture of her teacher. Pauline said:

> *"We were taught good manners, to care for and consider people, very disciplined really which carried me all through my life – courteous and kind."*

"We were taught good manners, to care for and consider people, very disciplined really which carried me all through my life – courteous and kind."

Pauline says that she learned to make pasties at her mother's side when she was six –"and haven't stopped since"! She also described making 'Pudding Skins' – pigs intestines, well washed and scoured, they were thin and stretched and stuffed with either savoury (suet and meat) or a dough with currents (sweet) and then roasted –"I used to hate them but I had to sit and eat them!"

Left: Mrs Rowe is a Bard of the Cornish Gorsedd.

Her reminiscences record life as it used to be – milk delivered by pony and trap, fresh food kept in the 'safe' – a perforated metal box kept outside the back door, the only fridge available in the 1930's, the His Masters Voice wind up gramophone. She remembers Tea Treat parades on Whit Monday in Camborne and Roskear Church visits to Carbis Bay beach – Pauline had a knitted bathing suit of Green wool, went swimming and the bathing suit stretched because of the weight of the water and was never worn again!! In the war she learned how to make a skirt for herself out of a pair of men's trousers.

"Mining was on the way out but we could hear the mines and the shafts around us. As the air was pumped through it would gush out of the shafts with a 'swoosh'. We could hear South Crofty quite plainly."

Mr Rowe had also travelled west – brought up on a farm the family moved from Four Lanes to Praze and Beeble and then to Tregender farm in Ludgvan. Steeped in agriculture all of his life he can still name all the fields on his farm. One particular memory was of 'possie piles'- seaweed and dung left in piles until rotted enough to be spread on the land. Pretty smelly apparently!

Mrs Rowe said that as a farmers wife :

"I worked hard but enjoyed it. I grew anemones and violets for the market, anything up to five women working with me. At busy times when the men were on the broccoli I would do the milking, separate the cream, scald it on the Aga in the kitchen to make butter for my own use. We used to feed the calves, raise the pigs and the calves. I was always doing something. When it got terribly busy, the seasonal work, a woman across the road came and did my housework for me. I would do the laundry and the cooking. Thrash days were a bit of a bind because I would have to do a lot of cooking for the croust time. The worst thing that could happen is that it rained on that day and I was left with all this food. Yes I have saved calves from certain death, revived dying pigs only of course to grow and be slaughtered which upset me. I used to raise poultry for Christmas and sell eggs and do all that. I did all my own decorating, papering and painting indoors"

Above: Crowlas in 1910

PEOPLE - PAULINE AND ALFRED JOHN ROWE

Bill Sewell

Eric William Sewell (born 1923), known to all as Bill is not a native of the area but has become very well known in the communities of Marazion and Perranuthnoe.

His grandfather worked on the railways and this brought him to Marazion for holidays and then to stay. Bill first visited the town when he was 6 months old. He grew up in Birmingham and when he left school took up an apprenticeship with Hangar Motors but at the start of the war the senior mechanics went off to fight and Bill was laid off. His grandfather got him an apprenticeship with the Shrapnel brothers (Mr. Clarence and Mr. Arthur) in their garage in the old drill hall, at the top end of Marazion.

Bill was called up and served in the REME in Egypt – he says that they had been trained to service British tanks and armoured cars but all the time he was in the Middle East only ever saw American equipment!

Demobbed in 1947, Bill returned to Marazion and joined the T F Hosking company as a mechanic – he worked for them for the next 40 years alongside colleagues such as Bobby Laity, Ronnie Kellow and Archie Godding.

He has very fond memories on Marazion during this period. He enjoyed visiting farms to maintain their tractors, he crewed for Arthur Hosking at the sailing club and remembers skating on Marazion Marsh – he fell backwards, hit his head and never went skating again! He served as part of the volunteer fire service when the engine was garaged underneath St Thomas' Hall and mixed with the soldiers billeted in the town, including some of the Americans. He tells the story of Alf Ramsey who later managed the World Cup winning English soccer team, getting up a team of soldiers to play the locals at the Football Club. However his Midlands roots are always reflected in many of his memories:

Bill Sewell in 1947 with the REME in Egypt, standing beside a Staghound Armoured Car.

> *"There were lots of shops in Marazion in the 1930's – you could buy anything. There was even a Banana Store owned by Mr. Baker who imported fruit and stored it in a corrugated iron shed with paraffin stoves to help the fruit to ripen, you could smell it from outside."*

"Mr. and Mrs. Calfe ran the paper shop. My grandfather had seen lots of poverty in the Midlands and was a strict socialist but Mr. Calfe was a Conservative and refused to sell the Daily Herald! Grandfather had to get his daily paper from W H Smith in Penzance – delivered by a boy on a bike."

Isabel Thomas

Isabel aged 20.

Isabel worked for Spirella for about thirty years. She trained as a corsetiere and travelled West Cornwall and even the Isles of Scilly.

"My husband saw an advert in the Paper and I went away and trained. Do you know that factory in Letchworth is now a listed building. I later became a consultant. In the early days they had stays of every description but they went out of fashion and Spirella went out of business in 1990. I had clients in Penzance where there were two in the same street and neither of them knew that they were clients – I was very proud of that. I had some very important people – but I am not going to tell you about them!!"

Isabel Thomas is a highly respected member of the Marazion Community. She has served on various committees and still attends as many events as possible, moving to the town in 1943. She was born in Regina, Canada in 1914 and her mother died when she was eight. Her father brought Isabel and her four brothers home to St Agnes, found homes for all the children before establishing himself and reuniting the family. This story of tragedy abroad and returning to the homeland is not uncommon amongst our recordings. Isabel first joined the Red Cross in 1935 and was called up in the Second World War as an Auxiliary at Redruth Hospital...

Isabel trained in Civil Defence before the Second World War. "That started when I was being trained, you had to do all these courses and learn about the gasses and learn first aid and go to these gas chambers and do exercises. We used to go out on exercises and they would pretend a bomb had dropped or something so you learned what to do. As an Instructor you would learn how to give people different tasks and get stuck in yourself of course if you had any sense. They used to do exercises over in Penlee Quarry. That all stopped after the War. There were ARP wardens in fact for a time I was an ARP Warden and used to go out when the siren went. We checked the blackout – I was the only woman in my area."

"I hadn't been in Marazion more than a month when I was brought into the Red Cross detachment which had just started up; it had previously been part of the Penzance Group. Francis Trudgen had been the quartermaster of the Marazion branch and became the Commandant of the new set up. It grew and grew. It was for women and girls who did the nursing courses and bit by bit they got called up to the war. We had both boy and girl cadets. We supported any charity and were often asked to collect for other groups. We had to buy our uniforms, paid for our badges and it got very expensive. I resigned in 1974 having served for 37 years, resigning as a Divisional Instructor responsible for three detachments- Penzance, Carbis Bay and Marazion. I came down here as a Civil Defence Officer, then Assistant Commandant, then Commandant. During our training we got called into hospitals to do ward duty and after the war we staffed Shows and Point to Point meetings. Penwith Red Cross was the first in Cornwall to have a ressuci-ann model"

Godfrey Varker

Godfrey is a true character – 80 years old and full of enthusiasm for Marazion and St Hilary. He was born in 1926 and named Geoffrey but every one knows him as Godfrey. Although from a local family his father was born in USA, Grandfather, a miner, had emigrated to Grass Valley and was killed in a mining accident in 1902 and Grandmother then brought the family back to St. Hilary.

Godfrey's father went back to the United States returning to St Hilary in 1925 where he set up business as a Carpenter, General Builder and Undertaker. – Father was quite entrepreneurial and even started a Taxi Firm, driving the same people to their weddings and funerals!!

Godfrey joined the firm at 14, paid "2/6d a week and all found". Father would pay out the wages to his workers on Saturday dinner times! Godfrey's father built a brand new bungalow next to his mothers house in Relubbus Lane in 1926 –

"The concrete blocks were made using waste from the local mine workings. Despite the newness, the bungalow had oil lamps, open fires and a Cornish Range. In 1948 father bought the decking from two corvettes and used this for fitting out the roof timbers and flooring of another new house. There was no mains water in the village but they dug an under ground rain water tank with an electric pump. Before this you could buy water, delivered by Mr. Harry Williams (known as Capt'n R) with his water butt pulled by his mule. The water was drawn from the pump at Relubbus and sold for 1d. a pail."

Godfrey's family were Chapel folk – Halamanning, Relubbus and Penburthy Cross mainly although there was a Chapel in every hamlet in the district. Chapel had a Harmonium and Sunday had a very strict routine – a tag end of Beef bought from Polglase, the mobile butcher, provided for the whole family for dinner, supper and the next day! Sunday School Tea Treat involved a visit from Camborne Band and a march from Hallamanning to Relubbus and back.

Godfrey was called up in 1945 – as a Bevan Boy and travelled to the coal mines on the Derbyshire/Nottinghamshire border – Eastwood, the home of D H Lawrence. Godfrey was there for three years, working with Pit Ponies supplying the coal seam which was only 3 feet high. Later he went to work on the coal face for £13 -10s a week. They were told to drink as much beer as they could to keep the dust down! He enjoyed this as he was not allowed to drink at home!!

He remembered:

- Charlie Williams who ran the village shop – serving butter, cheese, sweets and paraffin but had no wash up in the shop! Brook Bond tea was delivered by a van with solid tyres.

- John Paul James, Groom to the vicar at St Hilary who wore a bowler hat and leggings!

- Mr. King and Mr. Sedgemen, the well diggers who fell out while digging a well to supply water for Mr. Wilfred Rowe's Greenhouses at Halamanning and Mr. Sedgeman left Mr. King down the well! It was some time before he was found.

- The men of St Hilary institute who smoked clay pipes and used spittoons under the seats! As a boy Godfrey could watch the billiards but not allowed to speak!!

- Theirs was the first house in that area to have a phone in the 1930's. They had a sign outside 'YOU MAY PHONE FROM HERE'. People would come and pay for the phone but often they would wait to take a call, sitting for hours waiting for relatives to call, much to Godfrey's mother's distress.

Marie Vellanoweth

Marie Vellanoweth has lived all her life in Perranuthnoe. She was born in 1913 and spent her early life on the family farm. She and her mother moved off the farm in 1947 when her father died.

In our recordings she describes life in Perran before the war, the hard work of the farm when everything was done by hand and her education. She was an early driver, describing how she killed a 'fowl' when driving into the farm yard!! At 94 she was full of life and maintains a keen interest in the world around her including enjoying her computer and digital camera. When young Perranuthnoe was a farming community with the men fishing as a hobby and provided of food. It is now full of 'outsiders' second homes and seasonal shops – Marie's recording provides a vivid testimony of how one village has changed.

Marie told us some wonderful stories of her Grandfather. Grandfather was born in 1849 and died in 1944. He farmed all his life, helping on the farm until his death. We can only imagine how the world changed during his lifetime but Marie gives us some clues!! Up to his death everything on the farm was done by hand or with the aid of a horse. The family lived without mains water – water only arrived in Perranuthnoe in the 1950's and of course oil lamps and candles were the only source of light. The Cornish range or 'slab' was the great utilty source of heat and power and milk came straight from the cow. Making cream was a daily past-time.

Marie described life at home:

The cottage where she was brought up did not have any electricity or water. They collected rain water to fill a large tank sunk in the ground. The kitchen was large with an old fashioned slab and a table in the middle. They bathed in a galvanised Bath in front of the slab. The Toilet was outside and emptied by Dad. They had candles for light and stone floors in the kitchen. The family later had a radio – driven by accumulator batteries which were charged by Mr Basher in the garage at Goldsithney. Electricity came in the late 1920's. The Slab was replaced by a Welstead Cooker (like an Aga). In one of the outhouses was a large boiler used on washday to heat the water and clean the clothes. Irons had inserts which were heated in the fire and Fathers collars had to be starched and ironed. Water for the animals was brought in barrels from the adit at Trenowe but mains water arrived in the village around 1944. The family had a small market garden with some animals and made their own butter and cream. Groceries would be delivered.

Marie went to West Cornwall College when it was based in Chapel Street Penzance. The uniform was a navy blue tunic, black stockings, black shoes and a 'tusser' blouse. (silk) Marie would walk across the fields everyday from the village to Marazion station where someone from the school picked her up and took her to Penzance.

Marie did not have a huge social life. She left school at 14 and worked at home on the farm. The family

Marie's grandfather read the daily paper, predicted that Hitler was not to be trusted and was known affectionately throughout the village as 'Bobba'. However he could not come to terms with the telephone which he managed to answer but not engage in any conversation! Hardly surprising when he was born 50 years before the telephone was invented!!

Marie's Grandfather (born 1849) with his father.

attended the Chapel and the Sunday School and even in Marie's youth the numbers were small. There was a bus to Penzance once a week – on a Thursday. There was entertainment in Goldsithney such as dances at the 'Tin Tabernacle' but Marie was not allowed to go! She would swim from Boat Cove and her father built a tennis court behind the Church. She learned to drive during the war and would go to Penzance on a Saturday for Fish and Chips in Cherguin's Restaurant sitting in the window overlooking the street and then to the cinema or the Pavillion Theatre.

PEOPLE - MARIE VELLANOWETH 57

Father Walke

Much has been written and recorded about Father Walke the Vicar of St Hilary. Myra Kitchen a long living Goldsithney resident recorded her view of famous local priest:

"Father Walke – he was the finest man on God's earth. He practiced what he preached. People thought he may have been a bit strange in his religion at the start. He was high Church and some people objected to this – they were called the Kensites, some from Goldsithney. He had statues in the Church. I can remember that day that the church was tore up. We came out of school and walked through that way and the altar and everything was all broken up. It was devastating, dreadful. Going thought he avenue, in the wall I think its still there was a space and in that was a statue of the virgin Mary in a glass case and that was smashed to pieces. Some were local people.

He stayed for lots of years and then went to Mavagissy, its all written in 'Twenty years at St Hilary'[†] – I have a copy, limited edition. Some locals supported him. He was a wonderful man and he helped scores and scores of families.

He started an orphanage. I went to school with some of the children. That was over at what was the 'Jolly Tinners'. There was about 12 – 15 of them, there may have been more. He would bring them down from London, up in the slums and that. They were a lovely lot of children – one of them was a black girl, she was called Bernice, she had glasses, well in those days for a kid to wear glasses…….. They did not stay there but were there for lots of years.

He did a Christmas Play and also a Halloween one as well. I forget what it was called. I remember as a child going out into the street to hear the bells from the Church which were being recorded for the play on the radio. St Hilary Church bells were beautiful – every Tuesday night they would practice.

He was a wonderful, wonderful man. He was always on the road on his donkey – he once rode it as far as Lamorna!

[†] *Twenty years at St Hilary* by Bernard Walke - published by Truran

THE WAR

Throughout the project, from planning to completion, common themes emerged in the interviews we conducted. This section describes some of them.

SCHOOL

THE MOUNT

GROWING UP

Photography: Yvonne Oates

MARAZION MEMORIES

The Second World War

Our oldest interviewee was born in 1914 so we have few memories of the first world war, although some stories of parents during that conflict. However for most of our subjects 1939 – 1945 remain a very vivid memory. Some served, some were at school, some came to the area for the first time and many recollected the same stories! Details were some times vague but we gained an understanding of the essence of this period.

There was a great variety of activity and employment during the war but everyone was involved in the war effort in some way. Many of those involved in food production were in 'reserved occupations' and therefore could not go away but even so they usually served in the Home Guard, Fire watched or patrolled the coastal defences.

There was a gun above Marazion, a small garrison on the Mount and pill boxes around the coast. Women also supported the war effort by working but also through organisations such as the Red Cross and the WVS which ran a canteen in the Old Vicarage.

Many men were called up and we have heard stories of great escapades as well as bravery. The services also offered the men of the area the opportunity to

U.S. soldiers drill on Marazion Beach.

see parts of the world that they would otherwise never have seen. Without exception those we talked to had gained from the experience.

The Second World War saw Bevan Boys who were men conscripted to work in the mines. Some worked locally as mining still existed but others were shipped to the Midlands to work in the Coal Mines. In return many South Wales miners who were too unfit to continue mining came to Cornwall to work on the land. Surprisingly Italian (and some German) prisoners of war who were camped in St Erth also worked the land on many of the farms – we were told that the Germans were very good workers! Then there were the Land Army girls – many of whom stayed and married local farmers. The city girls had a steep learning curve but we have recordings explaining how welcome the families they stayed with made them. There was a hostel at St Hilary where many of them stayed and some were stationed on only one farm while others moved from farm to farm.

When we arranged for some of our subjects to be interviewed by the children the gap between reality and impression was found to be enormous. The youngsters got their views from film and TV but war time in West Cornwall was quite different. There were lots of soldiers, (particularly as D Day approached) in the area. The Inneskillen Fusiliers were remembered but the largest impact was from the Americans who were very friendly, had supplies of chewing gum and used the beach for exercises. Some kept contact with the 'yanks' and one recording describes a cross Atlantic wedding although it was believed by most we spoke with that the Americans based in the Town were in the first wave of Normandy Landings and the casualties were high.

Bombs were isolated but many remember bombs falling in Penzance with one family sheltering in the basement of Alfred Smiths when a raid began during a shopping trip! Two recordings describe the crash landing of an enemy aircraft and members of the Home Guard protecting the dead pilot until other authorities could deal with the situation. Apparently a Messerschmitt was displayed in Marazion Market Square as part as an appeal for War funds. The beaches were accessible but the main sands at Marazion had tank traps, barbed wire and mines. One subject remembered going over from the Folly Field to retrieve the football and safely returning although later a dog chasing a rabbit was not so lucky and got blown up.

Everyone remembers rationing but no one seems to have been short of food or gone hungry. In this area supplies were augmented from the sea, the countryside and of course gardens and allotments. People kept chickens and pigs and some suggestion of the 'black' market has been made to us. All schools had their own gardens and some of the senior boys at Marazion tended allotments and profits from the sale of the produce went to the war effort.

1942 - Enemy attack on Marazion

In recording several subjects we were told the story of the German plane which attacked the town in 1942. There were some variations in the account but basically one summers afternoon a German Plane came from the direction of Ludgvan and machine gunned or strafed the beach and the town. Among those who told us the tale were:

Lord St Levan:

"The Germans never bombed the Mount but they did machine gun the beach and the postman on the way back from the Mount had to hide behind Chapel rock - they were shooting at him"

Benny Lugg:

"Marazion got machine gunned – we were at school, I think that there was an air raid warning on – a fighter bomber went in and did some damage in St Ives and on their way back it strafed some farmers in the fields – it was harvest time I think and the council houses at the top a Mrs Jenkins and a Mrs Richards got injured with flying glass, not by the bullets."

George Curnow:

"Our class moved to the Methodist Sunday School around 1941-42. It was around 1942 that the Germans machine gunned the council houses and the school. We were down at the Sunday School so we were out of it but Henfor Close was shot and Mrs Richards and Mrs Jenkin got hurt with flying glass. At the school a friend of mine Gerald Hicks and my brother Gilbert, it was their last day at school and they were sent up to cut the grass on the cricket pitch and had to run for the hedge. Must have frightened the life out of them – but our class escaped the danger."

Bill Sewell:

"The Mount was machined gunned one evening – Harry Tomas and I were standing down on the car park and this Heinkle came over, it had bombed Penzance, and it finished up machine gunning the Mount Harbour. They did not do any damage but it put the breeze up people – they did it at several fishing ports including St. Ives. Marazion was shot up with Messerschmitt – they came over at low level, sea level and shot up Marazion, the top end of the town and there was a Mrs Jenkin who was expecting a baby and she got hit, she was out in the garden hanging out the clothes when these damn machines came over. That would be about 1941-42."

Two ladies were hit – one, Mrs Jenkins as she hung out her washing in her garden.

There follows an account from 2007 where her daughter Pam tells us the story:

"We lived at no 29, my Grandmother lived at 26. My mother was a wonderful woman and we nearly lost her in the war. My memory is that in those days we had evacuees and so every day certain classes had to go to the Sunday School for lessons. We were there and when I came home from school and got outside my auntie's house there was an ambulance there and a trail of blood going right across to my mothers house. I was 7 then. Mum was having morning sickness with my brother.

I went to my house and there was nothing there – all the windows had gone, there was not a pane of glass in the whole terrace. My father took me to my aunts as my mother was going into the ambulance. We had a neighbour called Mr Nicholls – she was late this morning putting the washing out she had an enamel bowl and Mr Nicholls shouted – go in Mrs Jenkin the gerries are coming – he could hear the plane.

She picked up the bowl, turned and the machine gun hit her – it cut the bottom of the enamel bowl she was holding right out, machined her right across the stomach. Our other neighbour, on the other side Mrs Richards she had 4 children, the youngest girl called Barbara and she was also hit across the bum – she Mrs Jenkin could not sit down for some time. But my mother was very badly hit. If it was not for the bowl she would not be here today.

She went into the hospital and my aunt looked after us as well as her own family. My mother was in hospital for 3, 4 even 5 months. The baby was fine – he's 64 next April!"

Pamela Triggs

Mrs Jenkin in 1938.

School

Reuben Collins returns to his Primary School 80 years after he first attended to reminisce about the happy time he spent there. The building still exists although modernised and adapted and his memories of the teachers and his peers are clear and informative.

Everyone remembers their school days. We have recorded many different accounts of what school was like but the common theme is that schools days are rarely forgotten. We have been told of good teachers, strict teachers, the classrooms, the lunch arrangements from walking miles home for a meal to the legendary lunches cooked by Mrs. Honey at Marazion School. The (particular difficulties and pleasures of attending school from the Mount when emergency arrangements for a billet on the main land which was often required and the jealousy of the other pupils when the Mount children were summoned home early because of an impending storm.

War brought a different situation with extra pupils and make-shift arrangements such as using the local Sunday school room (Marazion) and the memorable walk around the bomb crater in St Hilary!. Travel to school was an experience in itself – long walks in all weathers, the bus or train to the Grammar School in Penzance, the smell of wet clothing drying out on the classroom stove and some interviewees even confessed to missing the odd school session.

The curriculum before the Second World War was very broad with children still attending 'all through' schools until he late 1950's (although they did travel to special cooking (girls) and woodwork (boys) sessions). Some of the older subjects remembered the joys of nature walks or the excitement of leaving school at 14 to start work.

The project brought 5 former pupils to Marazion School to reflect on their memories of School. Starting school between the 1920's and 1950's their reminiscences described the changes in education over the 20th Century. They also described their fellow pupils, the dynamics of the school room and of course their own particular memories of significant events in their personal development. What was clear was that school was a very positive time for most and they all envied the quality of the buildings and opportunities that modern day pupil enjoy.

The project worked in all three Primary Schools in the Marazion Forum Area. At **St. Hilary** we collaborated with Alessandra Ausenda in bringing former pupils back to be interviewed by the present day pupils. The work with Sid Hayes (below left) and Mrs Kendall-Carpenter and Mr Allen (opposite) were very illuminating. Although the school had changed considerably the former pupils could still identify important areas of the school and describe events that they experienced. School was very different with no transport, no school dinners and very basic facilities but teachers made a vital impact of the quality of their experience and they all held a clear affection for their school. The pupils also showed a great interest in how school had changed and questioned and recorded their findings with a great respect for their visitors.

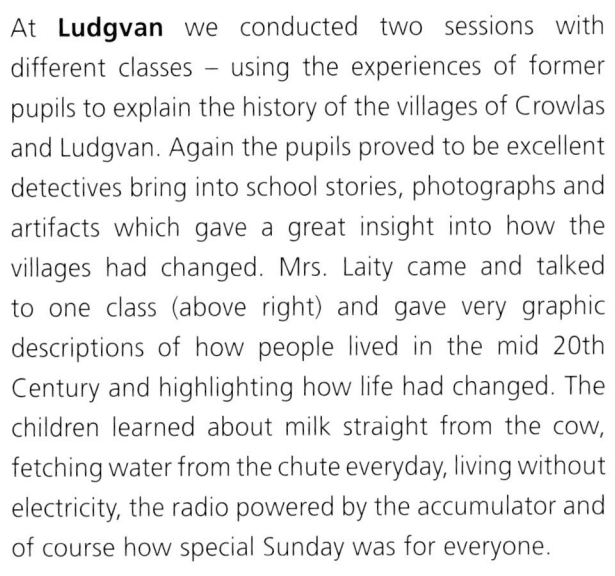

At **Ludgvan** we conducted two sessions with different classes – using the experiences of former pupils to explain the history of the villages of Crowlas and Ludgvan. Again the pupils proved to be excellent detectives bring into school stories, photographs and artifacts which gave a great insight into how the villages had changed. Mrs. Laity came and talked to one class (above right) and gave very graphic descriptions of how people lived in the mid 20th Century and highlighting how life had changed. The children learned about milk straight from the cow, fetching water from the chute everyday, living without electricity, the radio powered by the accumulator and of course how special Sunday was for everyone.

Marazion School was the focus of two pieces of work based in the Second World War. Again we brought together the older and younger generations and provided the pupils with the opportunity to research and investigate what life was like during the war. Their was some frustration amongst some of the senior citizens that the youngsters view of the war in Marazion was very unrealistic and they carefully explained that the town was not blitzed, those who lived there did not shoot a lot of the enemy and that despite some hardship everyday life continued as best it could. The children were fascinated and learned a lot.

Dorothy Round went to Marazion School in 1924. Her father was Headteacher. She now lives in California aged 86. She has recorded two volumes of memories; the following is an extract describing her early days at Marazion School.

After Christmas 1924, I was sent to school. I was four years and 4 months old. Dad took me to Miss Lambert's room, said 'be a good girl and do what Miss Lambert tells you now' and then he was gone!

Miss Lambert took my paper wrapped sandwich – for playtime- and put it on top of the high book cupboard with all the other little packages and her apple, well out of the reach of hungry boys. She showed me where to hang my coat and hat, in the cloakroom near the back door, and then gave me a seat in the 'babies class'. Second class was in the middle of the room and first class over on the far side. My seatmate was Monica Pearce, daughter of the village policeman.

School began with a hymn, Miss Lambert pumping out the time on the foot powered harmonium. Then she told us a Bible story and we repeated the Lords Prayer. Miss Lambert gave us a paper tub of yellow and brown seashells, the kind I liked to collect. This was all right! We were allowed to play with the shells –quietly -no talking- while she settled second and first classes with their sum books. Then she came back to us and told us to take 3 shells out of the tub and put them in a straight line. Sums were wonderful – sums meant playing with shells!! After playtime came reading.

The noon break lasted an hour and a half because some children had to walk a mile or two home. In the 1920's every child went home for dinner, rain or shine, storm wind or calm. The few students who came by boat at high tide, from the Mount, ate at a friends house.

Afternoon school was just as structured for the Infants as the academic morning lessons and discipline was never relaxed: however it was less studious. Miss Lambert read or told us a story, we sang to her harmonium accompaniment and depending on sex, we knitted or drew pictures. I don't remember that any little girl expressed jealousy over the fact that the boys could draw while we had to knit. Knitting was something that every girl had to do and no one dreamed of fussing about it.

How do you teach several four year olds to knit, all at the same time? Miss Lambert knew how. The girls in first and second classes need no help and worked industriously at their white cotton dishcloths using thick wooden needles. All the girls in the baby's class were told to stand, turn around, and sit on your desktops with your feet on the seat. Miss Lambert stood behind one little girl at a time and we all listened as she said the magic words that turned us into knitters." In – round –through –off. In round –through- off." Suddenly Miss Lambert had her arms around me, her plump bosom pushing against my back. She was holding a pair of knitting needles with a few rows already done. 'Watch me' she said. She stuck the right needle into the stitch on the left needle, saying' in'. She swung the thick cotton yarn around the needle as she said 'round' and then very slowly twisted the needle point as she said 'through' and slithered the old stitch off the needle point as she said 'off' She showed me twice Then she held her hands on mine and guided me through the process. Then she told me to try it myself and moved on the Monica.

Dorothy Round describes the toilet facilities at Marazion School in the 1920's:

After sums we packed away the shells and Miss Lambert handed us our 'lunch' and we went out into the yard to eat it and have playtime. At the top of the yard was an open fronted shed where we could get some shelter on rainy days. It was on the girl's side of the yard. The boys had no shed. It did not matter if the boys got wet; although if the weather was really bad we were allowed to have playtime in the classrooms. Just outside the shed was the dustbin where we put our sandwich papers, orange peel and apple cores. It had another use too as I found the first time I needed to 'go bizzy' at school. There was no toilet paper in the outdoor lavatories, as it was not considered necessary for children. I did not need it for pee- wee, but for 'bizzy' I needed paper.

I appealed to Kathleen Ivey who had started school the previous September and was in the second class already. She told me to look in the dustbin and find a piece of paper that did not have too much jam on it. I thought that's a fine idea and rummaged happily among the lunch papers. I knew how to crumple the paper and squeeze it hard to soften it before unfolding it to use on my bottom. I had been taught to do that with the pages from the National Union of Teachers directory for the previous year, which is what we used at home, till all the pages had gone. Then we had to buy toilet paper which in those days was just as stiff as the pages.

■ ■ ■ ■ ■ ■ ■ ■ ■ ■ ■ ■ ■ ■ ■ ■ ■ ■

Marazion School

Recorded 22 June 2005

John Allen

My unhappiest moments were when the school dentist came round. He brought his own chair which he set up in one of the classrooms and we all lined up and were examined! The other outside visitor was the lady who inspected us for nits! There was gardening up the back for the good boys – you could go and weed the Gooseberries. School was nothing like it is today.. Miss Floyd in the infants, then we moved up until the end we were in the top class with Ambrose. Ambrose's discipline was second to none. The division between his class and Mr Davey's was a curtain so you heard everything that was going on!

Reuben Collins

I started school in 1928 and even the old building looked different in those days. There was a big slope in the middle of the school and we used to slide down it in our hob nail boots to make sparks. One playground all the way around, no playing field at the back. We did not do any PE but played football everyday in the School Yard, wearing our hob nail boots – if you got a kick you knew it! Miss Lambert was in the Infants class – she was a lovely lady, then Miss Trevaskis. Punishment was strict, Miss Trevaskis would rap you with a ruler across the knuckles. There was no problem in the classroom. In the big room there was no curtain, Mr Round had class 6, 7 and 8 all in the same room. Each class had different work and how he managed it do not know. He would sit by the Cornish Range, we used to say he was warm while we were shivering. I spent two years in class 8 but I did not pass for the Grammar School. We used to have a preliminary but only one or two would get through the final exam. I left at 14 to go and work with Dad on the farm. The teachers were all great teachers and looked after anyone in trouble. Mr Round was a great naturalist and we would have a class of 'Bird and Tree' – each child would pick a bird and a tree and we would be sent out in the afternoons to sit in your tree and hope that the bird you picked was in the same tree!. I know one year I had an old alder tree and a blue tit and to get that blue tit to come to the elder tree was quite a problem. It was good to get out in the open. Swimming – Mr Round had a boat so we all went off Chapel Rock and that's where we learned to swim – I ended up with a hundred yards certificate! Dinner time was from 12 to half past one so we could walk home for lunch. John Trevorrow came from their Farm at Tregillion to get to school, that was the farthest and about two and half miles – he was often late but always had an excuse.

● **Howard Curnow**

I can remember in 1947, I must have been in the top class, Ambrose Richards (Head) called me out onto the top steps and took out his spy glass and we watched the Warspite. He described how they were trying to save the ship but later that day it went aground at Prussia Cove.

For dinners we used to sit in the bike shed and have sandwiches but on Tuesday senior boys would come around the school asking who wanted Fish and Chips and they would go down into the town to buy them for 6d. Thursdays they would do the same for Pasties at 6d.each. Then the new canteen was built – what a wonderful place! You had to go in there – total silence, no one dared to speak!

This school is coming up for its hundredth birthday. When the Parish of Marazion was created in 1895 they converted a 'Chapel of Ease' into the Parish Church. Behind there they had rooms where the girls went to school but they were in a bad state of repair with leaking roofs, so they moved to 'top town' to the new school for Girls and Infants which opened 1905. The boys were still in the old school in the Town but Mr. Round and the boys later moved up here as well.

Miss Warren made us learn 'I wandered lonely as a cloud that floats on high o'er vale and hill' and then she said – draw it!! Everyone drew hills and daffodils. Ambrose Richards came in and picked out mine and told the class that I had drawn the view through an open window – "all of you wandered on your feet, young Curnow wandered in his head, come out here boy "– and he gave me sixpence!

● **David Eddy**

I started school in 1944 and left aged 14. Wonderful days! Our headmaster, Mr Richards was a character. You were in a classroom doing lessons and if you were not paying attention he would slap the desk with two pieces of round elastic about a big as my thumb, like clap of thunder! Telfer Davey was a very good sports teacher. Miss Warren. Miss Trevaskis who became Mrs Vellanoweth and Miss Floyd - she was dear but a very strict disciplinarian. Of course we had outside toilets in the yard.

The Mount

The great iconic edifice nestling at the edge of the Bay named after it, the Island and Castle of St Michael's Mount is both separate from and part of the town of Marazion. Almost all of our recordings make some mention of the Mount and its connection with the people who live overlooking it.

Photo: Yvonne Oates

The individual accounts in this book give most of the testimony to the uniqueness of the place and many describe just how special it is. Most of the modern Royal Family have visited, apart from the Queen, and Queen Victoria set foot on the island with her devoted Prince Albert. The St Aubyn family have brought employment, wealth and some beneficence to the area with their extensive holdings of land and businesses. The present Lord St Levan is very much part of Marazion with his total commitment to local groups and organisations and his friendly presence in the Town. However earlier Lordships were more remote and at the beginning of the 20th Century very grand indeed – lots of servants and a distance maintained between the classes. However one thread has remained throughout the whole Baronetcy and that is the determination to maintain the building for its historical and visual importance and to sustain their tenancies to keep the land productive, agriculturally and financially.

St Aubyn Estate land stretches across the four Parishes of the project. Their annual Rent Court maintains a tradition of many generations and numerous interviewees testified to the support of the Estate in providing homes and farms. Renting from the estate provided jobs, opportunities and a degree of independence that would otherwise not have existed and the Manor Office has always been a key building in Marazion.

Living on the Mount marked people as 'different' in that all their activities were governed by the tides. Boatmen would go fishing before a days work in order to supplement their income and the Hobblers with their licences to ferry people to and from the Island saw themselves as quite special. George Curnow remembers ferrying Clark Gable (with one of the actor's cigarettes for his father) but the daily routine was more important. Getting water to the Castle demanded clever engineering, all the coal had to be hauled to the top of the Island using the supply railway, and every bit of food and furniture and personal belongings had to get to the top somehow! These days you can drive a Land Rover to the East entrance of the castle but not possible to take all the bends without manoeuvring. When the Queen Mother visited a special vehicle was purchased to carry her to the top without the need to reverse! It took a team of servants to service the Family and some accompanied them on their travels. Early in the Twentieth Century the Lordships were very grand with special trains to take them to London and many guests returning to Cornwall following the London season. His Lordship had a steam yacht, the St Michael which cruised the Cornish coast. The maintenance of the causeway was a continuous process with lime being spread on it in the early days to clear the weed and the little community huddled around the base of the island had to be fairly self sufficient because there were times when they were cut off. The Mount had its own fire fighting team and up to a few years ago a small fire engine. 5,000 gallons of water are stored under grounds on the island, there is a well half way up the path but they have had mains water since the 1930's. Re-laying the water main and new electricity and telephone cables proved problematical - the GPO laid their cable straight and the sand and sea moved it so much it kept breaking – whereas when it was 'snaked' with enough slack it was able to move with the shifting sands and remained intact.

Growing up on the island was later seen as a privilege – a close community, the freedom of roaming the Island and swimming in the harbour, the Christmas concerts in the presence of His Lordship and his visitors and of course many childhood pranks. We have been told of an annual cull of cats, a heard of cows, the Pub that was closed because a number of boatmen got drunk when Edward VII visited, never to open again, the old kitchens separated from the Dining room by a tunnel and the large number of employees in the middle of the last century.

The Warspite has also featured in many recordings. The beaching and breaking up of the ship on the sands in front of the town is etched upon people's minds. Many remember the towing around the bay, watching the drama unfold as it drifted ashore and of course the years as a rusting hulk. It has subsequently become very important to those who served on the warship who still return to the Town each year. His Lordship has wrecker's rights on Marazion Beach and the surrounding area if it could be seen from the tower of the Mount. There used to be branding irons used to mark salvage as the property of the family.

It was the salvagers working on the Warspite that first introduced the use of amphibious craft – the DUK. When they finished Lord St Levan bought one and they have been used ever since providing greater access to the island in all but the severest weather. In certain tides and winds the causeway can be out of use for many days – the longest we have been told is 5 consecutive days!

Frank O'Donnell

Marazion Memories has been priviledged to record Mr. Frank O'Donnell who was brought up on the Mount. Although his later childhood and working life was spent away from West Cornwall, he has returned to live in the area.

The following are reminiscences from his memoirs:

' St Michael's Mount, in the twenties and thirties was a unique, and for children, almost enchanted island. Not for us the fear of traffic or anything associated with human beings, we children knew everyone on the island and they knew to whom we belonged. There were of course the natural hazards of living on an island, the sea itself, stormy weather, climbing the cliffs and trees; but if the truth be told all those activities and dangers only served to make the mount a true paradise for a group of young children.

All of us had fallen into the sea more than once, the more adventurous of us on many occasions, either from the rocks on the seaward side or from the harbour wall while fishing. as far as the islanders were concerned the sea was a provider and there to be enjoyed. We were certainly taught to treat it with respect but it held no fear for us.

Everything about island life, pre-war was totally different to that of our friends and relatives on the mainland. The dominating feature was of course the weather. Our normal way of getting to school was by being rowed across in the small 'post boat' by Postman John.

Lord St Levan.

We were privileged to record Lord St Levan who remembered visiting Marazion for the Summer Holidays when he was a boy. His great uncle was the 2nd Baron St Levan and everyday they would go sailing on his yacht. His parents moved to the Mount in 1940 when his father inherited the title. Life on the Mount has changed over the last 50 years and is much less grand these days, although many traditions such as the Rent Court have been maintained. His Lordship believe that any historic house should play a part in the community and he is very well respected and fondly admired for his consistent support of Marazion and its organisations.

His Lordship told us many fascinating stories:

- There is a cemetery on the Mount – everyone who lived on the Island can be buried there as well as some sailors drowned off the island. There was no room for the ladies of the St Aubyn family so his aunts were buried at Gulval– so if they rose from the dead the first view they would have would be the Mount!

- Two cannon were stolen from the Castle ramparts by a group of French who moored their yacht behind the Mount and climbed the hill in the night. The family were concerned that Scotland Yard did not respond quickly enough to alert the French authorities and the family advertised in French Newspapers for its return!

- About 35 people live on the Mount and the houses have all been modernised. Before he inherited the title there were not many visitors to the Mount – this has increased, including the wonderful gardens. His father had been anxious not to commercialise the Mount.

- St Michael's Mount is a Parish in its own right. The monastery was there before William the Conqueror. They have their own Chaplin, independent of the Bishop of Truro and an 18th Century Organ in the Chapel.

- Many Royalty have visited - never the Queen or Prince Charles. But The Queen Mother, Princess Margaret, Duke of Kent, Duke of Gloucester etc. they once had a visit from the present Emperor of Japan when he was a student. On Easter Sunday they sent him to visit the music students at Prussia Cove, apparently the Japanese students were very frightened to meet him because he was regarded as a God!

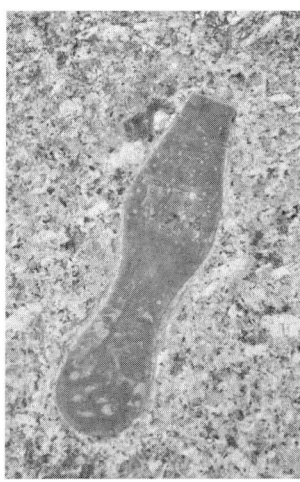

Queen Victoria's footprint on The Mount harbour pier.

- The Mount Dairy was built in Victorian times and modelled on the kitchen at Glastonbury Abbey. Used until 1930's. There were 6 cows kept on the Island.

- In 1725 the Tin Miners rioted and attacked the Granary on the Mount but largely in the 18th Century the St Aubyn family did a lot to help the miners by employing as many as possible. There was an 18th Century scandal that the 5th Baronet's children were not legitimate. He had 11 children by the same woman and only married her when they had all grown up. His cousin's family took all the best pictures but left his branch of the family to keep the *'Mount as a Monastery'* as it was not seen as very valuable!

- The St Aubyns Estate has been going since the 13th century and they still hold the Rent Court where in former times tenants paid their rent. However the traditional lunch is still held and the same families were there in 1947 and still there in 2005! The Court is 'men only' and has been held for at least 200 years!

Growing up

One of the greatest differences between the generations is how childhood has changed. The project did a great deal of work with youngsters in the area and managed to bring the old and young together in a number of ways. Details of these projects are contained in the newsletters we published but it was clear that our elder citizens were very keen to share how life has changed during their lifetime and how their stories interested the younger people.

Many differences between growing up in the first half of the 20th Century with doing the same in the first half of the 21stC

In the 1920's and 30's life was good but material things were not as plentiful - a Christmas stocking with a book, one toy and an orange was very welcome and exciting but would seem quite meagre to today's children.

Life two generations ago was very free - the school curriculum was flexible, nature walks and gardening were all well remembered as well as afternoons on the beach. Whole summers were spent as groups

Marazion Girls' School Copy Book 1908-1920.

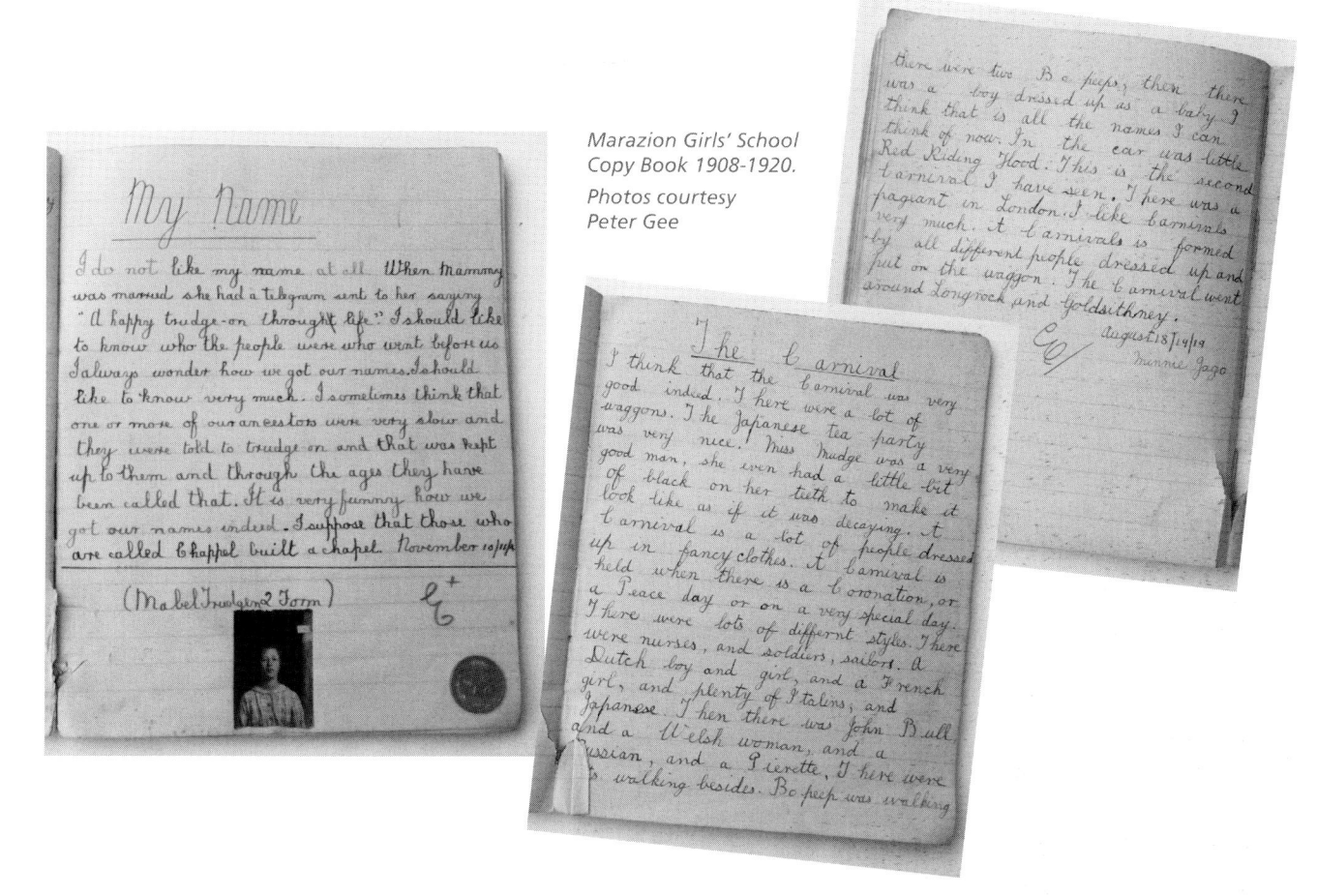

Photos courtesy Peter Gee

swimming and playing and the countryside was a large and very accessible playground. There was lots of what was described to us as 'mischief' and a clip around the ear from the village Bobby was enough to keep everyone in line, mainly because everyone knew everyone else.

Children encountered work very early in their lives. If you lived on a farm then working in the fields, tending the animals and generally helping was part of everyday life. Many cottages lacked mains water so fetching it from the local well or chute was children's work as was collecting milk from the local farm on a daily basis. School ended at 14 before the 2nd World War and 15 afterwards and although many gained scholarships to the Penzance Grammar Schools or paid to attend Hayle Grammar School, most children attended schools all the way through from 5 - 14. We have recorded several accounts of leaving school one day and starting work the next and coping with hard and physically demanding jobs at a very young age. Study was less of an option than today and the work was very restricted - farm work, shop work, for some learning a trade. The St Aubyn Estate was very important in providing employment as was the fact that lots of tasks were labour intensive with farms relying on hand work.

THEMES - GROWING UP

We also discovered that travelling long distances to work were not unusual - Goldsithney to Hayle for instance. Long walks to school in all weathers were also a feature of our recordings with housewife's proving lunch for all the family either at school or work or at home. We heard many vivid memories of drying clothes on the school stove! Walking was a normal form of transport - to church three times on a Sunday, to school each day and to various events around the district. There were buses but for many even these were expensive luxuries.

Houses of course changed greatly as well. No electricity for some they grew up with candles and oil lamps, no central heating for anyone, coal and wood fires and the slab or Cornish range became the centre of home life. An earth closet down the garden, the use of a tin bath tub once a week and mothers working long hours on a Monday to clean the clothes and then even more hours to iron them with flat irons. Clothes were not plentiful but most had a Sunday Best for special occasions. Entertainment developed with the first radios powered by batteries and firmly controlled by the man of the house but it did open up new horizons - boxing commentaries from America, plays from London and news from a whole new world. Other entertainments were often church based -choirs, film shows, concert parties were regular performances with many visiting the picture houses of Penzance once a week. Carnivals also featured in our recordings and seem to have covered every village and hamlet - dressing up and parading was great fun and the local brass bands always led the way.

We have not recorded a lot about the uniformed organisations such as the Girl Guides. We do know there was a scout group in Marazion in the 1930's and the Red Cross Detachment attracted girls well into the 1950's. Some Chapels had youth groups and there was a district wide system of visiting each others groups once a month. We learned little of the tensions of the teenage years or the generation gap and certainly the subjects we recorded who grew up in the 30's 40's and 50's were very obedient and non rebellious - or so they said to us!! Childhood may have been simpler for this group but it was also shorter. Education was acknowledged and tolerated by all but few described the benefits of school, just the fond memories. Several of our subjects were educated beyond the 15 year old school leaving age but local employment was usually the ultimate goal.

We have been told many funny stories about teachers - certainly school children 50 years ago were as naughty and mischievous as at any time. However most memories were positive and corporal punishment was accepted as the norm. What does come across is the teachers at the local school as important members of the local community, influential characters, and sometimes remembered in the most amazing detail.

One interviewee explained:

"I went to St Hilary School, but I never went very much because I had to work at home on the farm. When I was six I used to come home from school, have something to eat, perhaps a piece of bread because we did not have very much and then go and work in the orchard all evening. I dug around each tree and then when father came home we pulled them over. The next day I had to cut up the wood. Clearing the trees took months and then I had to dig over the new meadow - about half an acre - all by hand. By the time I was seven I was able to plough - a single plough pulled by a cob and at nine years of age I could handle a couple of shire horses!"

Our Partners

The project worked with many groups and organisations and are grateful to all for their collaboration, support, companionship and expoertise.

Allesandra Asunda
Francesca Asunda
Staff and pupils of Marazion School
Staff and pupils of Ludgvan School
Staff and pupils of St Hilary School
Mary Tudor
Jane Howells
Sheila Berriman
Graham and Sylvia Ronan
Kirsty Jones - Sure Start Chy Carn
Fiona Young - Geevor Mine
Alison Weeks - Porthcurno Wireless Museum
Marazion Town Museum
The Manor Office - Marazion
Mandy Morris and Garry Tregidga - CAVA
David and Carol Eddy
Michael Ball
Helen Wheatley - Heritage Lottery Fund

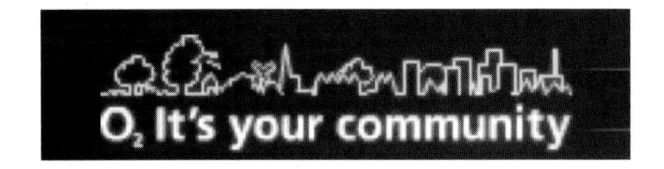

Heritage Lottery Fund

O₂ It's your community

Index

Ager, Stanley	34	Charter Fair	31	Education Office	46	Holman Brothers	48
Alessandra Ausenda	66	Cherguin's Restaurant	57	Elm Farm	9	Holmes	14
Alfred Smiths	62	Chichibu, Prince	14	Fairfield	47	Home Guard	18, 20, 27, 38, 44, 62
Alldale	38	Christmas Play	58	Fanshaw, Mr	31	Honey, Mrs	65
Allen, Arthur	16	Church Drama Group	41	Fire Engine Pub	25, 44	Hosken, Arthur	14, 31, 44
Allen, John	16	Church Hill	46	Flemington	14	Hosken, Francis	14, 44
Allen, Mr	66	Church Town	11	Floyd, Annie	23, 24	Hosken, Pearl	38
Allen, PC	13	Churchtown	46	Floyd, Marjorie	23	Hosking, Arthur	51
Andrewartha, John	36	Churchtown Farm	9	Floyd, Miss	71, 72	Inneskillen Fusiliers	62
Andrews, Cecil	39	Chy an Dour	33	Folly Field	41, 62	Intelligence Corps	30
Angwin, Mr	46	Chy Morvah	42	Four Lanes	49	Ivey, Gerald	24
ARP Warden	20, 53	Civil Defence	53	Fox, George	31	Ivey, Kathleen	71
Art School Penzance	46	Clipper Café	41	Freddy Reynolds Picnic Grounds	42	J Laity, Lt.	38
Ashton	29	Clontarf	9	Gable, Clark	75	Jackson, Mr	46
Axworthy, Miss	46	Coastguard Station Marazion	42	Germoe	29	Jago, Walter	24
Baker, Billy	14	Cobham's Flying Circus	37	Gibson, Miss	26	James, Joe	27
Baker, Mr	51	Cockbain, Averil	29	Gilbert, Mr	9	James, John Paul	55
Bamber, Sam	26	Colenso Farm	18	Gilbert's Yard	9	Jenkin, Nicky	27
Banana Store	51	Collins, Sam	24	Glass, Maj.	27	Jenkins, Mrs	63
Barber Hocking	41	Cook, Howard	43	Godding, Archie	50	Jewell, John	24
Basher, Dickie	31	Cooks Landing	43	Godolphin Company	43	Jewell, Roy	14
Basher, Mr	57	Cornish Range	11	Godolphin Hotel	42	Jones, Amy	46
Beard, Victor	31	Cornwall Audio and Visual Archive	3	Godolphin Steps	14	Jones, Mr	46
Bennett, Mr	43	Cornwall Constabulary	16	Goldsithney School	30	Jordan, Miss	31
Bennetts, John	31	Cornwall Religious Drama Federation	29	Grass Valley	54	Keeve	36
Berrimans Bus	23, 27, 33, 37	Corpus Christie Fair	33	Groft Gotha	38	Kellow, Ronnie	50
Bethlehem Play	7, 32	Crowlas	11,12, 29, 37, 46, 67	Guard, Annie	47	Kendall-Carpenter, Mrs	66
Bettens, Mr	9, 33	Culley, Jimmy	41	Gulval	77	Kenneth Bennetts, Dr.	28
Bevan Boy	24, 54, 61	Curnow, Freddy	46	Halamanning	54	Kensites	58
Bible Class	14	Curnow, George	75	Halamanning Park	39	Kestle Farm	33
Blissett, Frank	24	Curnow, Laura	10	Hall, Dick	24	King Edward VII	75
Blowing House Hill	46	Curnow, Mr	31	Halloween Play	58	King, Mr	55
Boat Cove	10, 57	Curnow, Percy	10	Hammill, Mrs	46	King, Sam	38
Bob, Charlie	30	Dale, Alice	38	Hangar Motors	50	Kliskies	27
Bonnet, Grace	38	Darby, Mr	47	Hansen, Mr	31	Kott, Peggy	28
Burrows, Rodney	27	Davey, Mr	71	Harris, Ermantrude	26	Laity, Bobby	50
Calf, Mr	14	Devon and Cornwall Light Infantry	24	Harvey, Blight	9	Laity, Dick	14
Calf, Philip	26	Dobson, Frank	10	Hayes, Sid	66	Laity, Jim	9
Calfe, Mr	51	Drop Anchor	10	Hayle Grammer School	46	Laity, Joe	9,10
Camborne Band	54	Dubban Farm	9	Hayle Merrymakers	37	Laity, John	9
Cape Cornwall Costumes	29	Duke of Cornwall Light Infantry	33	Henfor Close	63	Laity, Nicky	27
Care, Theophilus	14	East Pool Mine	24	Heritage Lottery	3,4	Laity, Willaim Joseph	9
Castle an Dinas	21	Eastern Green	17	Hicks, Gerald	63	Laity, William	10
Castle Gate	11	Ebenezer Chapel	42	Highfield, Rev	14	Lambert, Miss	69, 70, 71
Chapel Rock	14	Edmonds, Miss	30	Hill, George	14	Lamorna	9
Chapel Street	21	Ednovean	9	Hocking, Frederick Walford	42	Land Army	7, 13, 18, 61

i

Lanyon, Dickie	43	Pay Day	10	Rosudgeon	37	Trevorrow, John	72
Lawrence, Jimmy	42	Pearce, Clarry	14	Round, Dorothy	69	Triggs, Pamela	64
Lemin, Honor	38	Pearce, Miss	14	Round, Mr	13, 26, 71, 72	Trudgen, Francis	53
Lemin, John	38	Pearce, Monica	69	Rowe, Wilfred	55	Truro Butterflies	37
Leys Lane	41, 42	Penalyree House	9	Royal Enniskillen Fusiliers	42	Truthwall	24, 43
Lister, Maj.	27	Penburthy Cross	54	Rundle, Mr	26	Uren, Johnny	43
Littler, Lt. S	38	Penlee Quarry	53	Sailing Club	44	Uthno-Veor	9
Local Defence Volunteers	27	Penny, Dr.	26	Saint Ludwan	12	Varker, Eddie	38
Long Lanes	37	Penwith District Council	5	Saint Paul	12	Vellanoweth Valley	11
Long Rock	11, 46	Penzance County School	10	Scanlon, Terry	24	Vellanoweth, Dick	31
Lower Kenneggy	24	Penzance Grammer School	26, 30, 41, 65	Seale Hayne Agricultural College	30	Vellanoweth, Marie	9
Lower Quarter	11	Perfect, Joe	30	Sedgemen, Mr	55	Vellanoweth, Mrs	72
Lower Quarter Fair	11	Perran Cross Roads	9, 37	Shop Hill	14	Venton	42
Ludgvan Fair	47	Perran Downs	22	Shrapnel Brothers	50	Venton View	44
Ludgvan Rectory	12	Peters, Nick	32	Sidney, Dr	28	Verran, Mr	46
Ludgvan School	21	Phillips, Arthur	14	Smasher Louis	42	Virgin Hill	27
Lynfield	9	Plain-an-Gwarry	32	South Crofty	49	Wagner, 'Boss'	46
Mallenear	46	Polglase	54	Spirella	52	Wagner, Edith	46
Marazion Busses	27	Police Gazzette	17	St Aubyn Estate	18, 19	Walke, Bernard	7, 32
Marazion Fair	44	Powell, Jimmy	24	St Aubyn, Miss Hilaria	26	Wall	24
Marazion Market Square	62	Powers, Gary	30	St Erbyns	30	WARAG	20
Marazion Marsh	51	Praze an Beeble	49	St Erth	26, 61	Warden, Dolly	41
Marazion Scout Group	44	Primrose Hill	31	St Thomas' Hall	51	Wardens Printers	41
Marazion Station	10, 18, 20	Prince Albert	74	Stanhope Forbes	38	Warren, Miss	23, 72
Marazion Town Band	42	Prussia Cove	24, 72, 77	Star Inn	46	Warspite	72, 76
Marriot, Clive	27	Queen Mother	75	Stevens, Roy	24	West Cornwall School	21
Martin, Ernie	24	Queen Victoria	74	T F Hosking	25, 41, 50	White Hart	12
Matthews, Willie	44	Quinn, Laurie	37	Tea Treats	7, 11, 37, 48, 54	White, Bertie	43
Minack Theatre	29	Ramsey, Alf	51	The Defender	46	White, Capt.	38, 44
Mitchells Printers	41	Red Cross	53, 60	The Wardrobe	29	White, Roy	14
Moon Family	11	Reid, Mr	46	Thomas, Harry	63	Williams, Arnold	14
Mudge, Jack	26	Relubbas	23, 38	Tin Tabernacle	57	Williams, Charlie	55
Mudge, Jim	14	Relubbus Carnival	7	Tonkin, Mr	42	Williams, Ernie	14
Murley, Canon	12	Relubbus Lane	54	Townsend, Lady	36	Williams, Francis	38
Nancledra	46	Rent Court	19, 75	Tregender Farm	49	Williams, Harry	54
Nash, Miss	30	Reynolds, Tom	14, 37, 47	Tregillion	72	Wimbledon, Miss	46
National Service	30	Richards, Ambrose	23, 71, 72	Tregurtha Mine	38	Women's Institute	12
New Town, Marazion	42	Richards, Francis	14	Trembath, Lucy	46	WVS	60
Nicholls, Mr	64	Richards, Miss	14	Trembath, Sid	24	York House	21
Ninns, Miss	46	Richards, Mrs	63, 64	Trenow Beach	10	Young Wives Group	12
Oates, Victor	23	Richards, Teresa	37	Trenow Quarry	10	Young, Finson	32
Old Cornwall Society	11	Robinson, Robert	34	Trenowe	57		
Padereski	14	Rodda, Jimmy	24	Trevarthian Farm	18		
Park-an-Praze	9	Roskear Church	48	Trevaskis, Miss	23, 71		
Parkins Shop	26	Rospeath	43	Trevaskis, Willie	24		
Pavillion Theatre	57			Trevelyan Arms	31		